es

CAN WOMEN

BE

GENTLEMEN?

BOOKS BY MRS. ATHERTON

Fiction

(California)

REZÁNOV
THE DOOMSWOMAN
THE SPLENDID IDLE FORTIES (1800–1846)
A DAUGHTER OF THE VINE (The Sixties)
TRANSPLANTED (The Eighties)
THE CALIFORNIANS (Companion Volume to Transplanted)
A WHIRL ASUNDER (The Nineties)
ANCESTORS (Present)
THE VALIANT RUNAWAYS: A Book for Boys (1840)
SISTERS-IN-LAW (The Present)
SLEEPING FIRES (The Sixties)
THE AVALANCHE

(In Other Parts of the World)

THE FOGHORN (Four Stories)
THE WHITE MORNING
MRS. BALFAME
PERCH OF THE DEVIL (Montana)
TOWER OF IVORY (Munich and England)
JULIA FRANCE AND HER TIMES (B.W.I. and England)
RULERS OF KINGS (Austria, Hungary and the Adirondacks)
THE TRAVELING THIRDS (Spain)
THE GORGEOUS ISLE (Nevis, B.W.I.)
SENATOR NORTH (Washington)
PATIENCE SPARHAWK AND HER TIMES (California and New York)
THE ARISTOCRATS (The Adirondacks)
THE BELL IN THE FOG (Short Stories of Various Climes and Places)
BLACK OXEN (New York)
THE CRYSTAL CUP (New York and New Jersey)
THE IMMORTAL MARRIAGE (Ancient Greece)
THE JEALOUS GODS (Ancient Greece)
DIDO: QUEEN OF HEARTS (Tyre and Carthage)
THE SOPHISTICATES
GOLDEN PEACOCK

Autobiography

ADVENTURES OF A NOVELIST

War

THE LIVING PRESENT

History

THE CONQUEROR
A FEW OF HAMILTON'S LETTERS
CALIFORNIA: AN INTIMATE HISTORY

Essays

CAN WOMEN BE GENTLEMEN?

CAN WOMEN

BE

GENTLEMEN?

BY

GERTRUDE ATHERTON

HOUGHTON MIFFLIN COMPANY · BOSTON

The Riverside Press Cambridge

1938

The Riverside Press
CAMBRIDGE · MASSACHUSETTS
PRINTED IN THE U.S.A.

TO

B. A. BERGMAN

WITH PLEASANT MEMORIES

A clever man asked me three questions: Are women born liars? Why have so few women the instincts of gentlemen? Why do women hate one another? I have answered these questions in the following three chapters according to my lights (not his!).

CONTENTS

CAN WOMEN

BE

GENTLEMEN?

... How in all points their lives obey the law
Of Egypt, where the men keep house and weave,
Sitting within-doors, while the wives abroad
Provide with ceaseless toil the means of life.

SOPHOCLES, *Oedipus at Colonus*

In the course of two hundred and fifty years thirteen
Ptolemies had succeeded one another, governed or perse-
cuted by their women, like the Pharaohs, their predecessors on the Nile.

EMIL LUDWIG, *Cleopatra*

CHAPTER I

ARE WOMEN

BORN LIARS?

WHAT a fertile subject! And how differently
it would have been answered thirty years ago.

Leaving aside the amoral and the congenital
romancers, both men and women with few exceptions
lie from one of two motives: politeness, which includes the desire to please, and fear, which is often
inspired by self-interest, notably in the case of politicians. Were the polite lie abolished the now well-
oiled wheels of society would rust, crack, fall to
pieces, and hatred would become the ruling passion.

As to fear. Men lie to women for the sake of
peace or to accomplish some nefarious end. But in
the business and professional world they know their
word must be indubious or they will be edged out
of the struggle for supremacy, or mere existence.
Self-interest alone would make them normally
truthful.

But women. Those who for centuries were known
as the weaker sex. Without political or economic
rights, tyrannized over by fathers, husbands, often

3

by grown sons, only the nonentities succumbed utterly. The vast majority brought lying, deceit, circumvention, to a fine art. The arrogance of the male, too powerful to find lying a necessity, was not for them. Inevitably, with rare exceptions, they were the inferiors of the male in character as in stature. And by force of habit they lied as freely to one another as to their household tyrants.

But as time passed the more intelligent resented their ignominious position, not only as the mere creatures of the all-conquering male, but the lack of opportunity to develop independence of mind and nobility of character. Finally the great movement for what was then called emancipation began.

I have no intention of recapitulating the long struggle for the franchise in the nineteenth century and its victory in the twentieth. That story is too well known.

Let us take a long curve backward into the fifth century B.C.

All who have read 'The Dominant Sex' by Mathilde and Mathias Verting, profound scholars who quote authorities both ancient and modern, know that for centuries women were the ruling sex in Egypt. They were also dominant in Germania, Libya, certain minor states. In the sixth century B.C. and well into the fifth they were dominant in Sparta. Athens is believed to have been a gynocracy in pre-Homeric times.

But we will confine ourselves to Egypt, where the Vertings make clear that women had ruled since the fourteenth century B.C.

4

Man was the subordinate sex. His position was that of women in the Athens of the fifth century, and later in the Christian era — until after long centuries of male dominance they found, in the middle of the nineteenth century, able and determined leaders in Elizabeth Cady Stanton and Susan B. Anthony, and the ominous revolution began.

Who the men were that led the rebellion in ancient times we have no record, but certain it is that even before the invasion of Alexander the Great and the Ptolemaic Dynasty the men of Egypt had grown increasingly restive and resentful and forced the female tyrants to grant them some measure of equality. There were already male artisans and merchants.

In the fifth century B.C. the women of Egypt transacted all the business of the state. They went forth every morning to the Market Place, engaged in commerce, banking, law, agricultural problems, and such international relations as they found it impossible to avoid. The husbands stayed indoors and looked after the home. Men were cooks, chambermaids, nurses, and what-not. Unless too dispirited, the husbands followed the example of male harlots, curled their hair and beards, scented themselves, used paint and kohl freely, practised all the little arts and graces peculiar to women elsewhere and of the centuries to follow.

There was just one thing the dominant sex could not impose upon men and that was the bearing of children. In this respect, only, was Nature too much for them. But they arose on the third day and went forth to attend to business while the husband went to bed with the baby to keep it warm. No amount of research has discovered whether the mother condescended to return at intervals to nurse her offspring, or if the family cow was requisitioned. But it would be quite in keeping that she nursed the girls and the father brought up the boys on the bottle.

But in no other respect were those women the victims of Nature. It has been demonstrated by the Vertings that aside from mere sex there is no biological difference between men and women. Those ancient females were tall and strong, as powerful in body as in mind, whereas the men were inferior both in physical and mental development. The women lived their days in the open air, exercised vigorously; from childhood they had been more adequately nourished than the male. The men lived the indoor life, received no physical training, accumulated fat, were permitted to occupy their minds with nothing beyond their household duties and the rearing of children. No doubt they met and gossiped, indulged in sly flirtations or liaisons, became expert in lying, and deceiving their over-ladies.

In Germany skeletons of women seven feet long have been unearthed. Whether Egyptian women ever attained this imposing height is not known, but contemporary historians testify to their fine physique and arrogance of carriage.

Permit me to imagine myself an Egyptian Woman of Importance in the fifth century B.C.

I arise at dawn, go to the bath, put on my severe

6

garment without folds, an ugly garment exactly like that of all the other women, but adapted to active life in the Market Place.

After a frugal breakfast I open a door and regard my husband, who is making his morning toilette before a bronze mirror. He is a pretty little thing with curling hair and beard, which I suspect him of treating with henna; it has acquired a reddish tinge of late. Not that I mind, for I am extremely tolerant, and after all it is a harmless manly weakness. He has lost the rosy complexion of youth, which he would restore with cosmetics, but here I draw the line. No husband of mine shall look like one of those harlots that lurk about the streets on the lookout for unfaithful wives who would keep them in luxury. I tell him I am satisfied with him as he is, and, indeed, I am quite fond of my dutiful little husband, and it is rarely I have occasion to knock him about; never, really, except when I catch him gorging the boys: economy must be practised in every household and the best, naturally, given to the girls. Or if I catch him sneaking into the house and he protests he has been worshipping in the Temple when I know full well he has been gossiping in some neighboring villa. Otherwise we are happy enough, for I am a woman of stern principles and quite faithful to him. Life is too busy for dalliance.

As I wish him a pleasant good morning he rises, drops on one knee, and bows his head. I raise him graciously and ask after the baby — our fifth.

7

'He had colic in the night and I walked the floor with him that you should not be disturbed. Now he sleeps, but if he should be attacked again may I call in the medico?'

I give an indifferent consent, and ask after my two fine girls, an unnecessary question as I hear their robust voices shouting in the court. But one I always ask, as a reminder that my vigilance never sleeps. My husband assures me eagerly that they are well and already so strong they have kicked their nurses black and blue. Well satisfied I drop a negligent kiss on the timidly uplifted brow and go forth to attend to more important matters.

My spacious villa is some distance out of town, but I cover the distance with long womanly strides. I throw back my broad shoulders and draw in long breaths of the sparkling air. The life-giving Nile flows along with a deep sweet murmur. Temples to Isis and lesser goddesses, statues, pyramids, and little sphinxes, remould the flat landscape. From all the temples within hearing comes the chanting of priestesses adoring their goddess. In imagination I see far away in the desert the great pyramids of Gizeh, and the famous Sphinx, whose austere visage I am proud to say is an exact reproduction of an ancestress, one of the queens of Egypt. For many generations now we have forsworn queens, who grew too ambitious and split the country into factions. A king is our nominal ruler. He does as he is told by a council of women, but is permitted to build temples and call them by his name. This gratifies his vanity and keeps him contented. We want neither scandals nor attempted revolutions.

The Market Place is a large irregular square surrounded by ornate buildings devoted to law, commerce, banking, an imposing Council Chamber, private offices, shops, and bazars.

It is already swarming, for the harbor is full of ships, and men have come from far lands to buy and sell. But I notice at once a group of women whose position in the city is as important as my own, and they seem to be conferring with unusual gravity. I join them at once. With anxious brows they inform me that Ethiopia is threatening to make war upon us, and that we must reinforce our mercenary troops of men. We are a peaceful nation and are seldom embroiled in war, but there is always danger from savage hordes and we keep a small standing army of foreign mercenaries. The Libyan women do their own fighting, like those mythical Amazons, but the women of Egypt have no taste for hardships and brutalities, see no reason to make beasts of themselves when they can hire men who live for nothing else. The King may lead the troops to battle if he wishes. It makes him feel important and less inclined to rebel at his impotence in the state.

We adjourn to the Council Chamber and send for the Captain of the Mercenaries. He arrives in haste, a great hulking fellow whose eyes flame with the lust of battle and increase of pay. Nevertheless, he stands before us in an attitude of extreme respect, takes our orders to send several of his men to neighboring states for additional troops, is given a sack of money, which he slings over his shoulder, and departs without presuming to utter a word.

I am not only a member of the Council but a woman of business, and when the others adjourn to the Palace to go through the formality of informing the King that a possible war impends, I cross the Market Place to the Hall of the Merchants. Here for several hours I am hearty and breezy, shrewd and calculating, and in eight cases out of ten getting the best of the bargain.

As I leave the Hall and am about to cross the Place, I notice a young man standing by one of the pillars. He is watching the bustling crowd of women, and foreign men from the ships, with a satiric expression, which changes, as he meets my disapproving eye, into one of defiance and resentment. Nor do his eyes fall before mine.

I had seen him before hanging about the Market Place and wondered who he was. An Egyptian certainly, but as he was neither scented nor painted it was evident that he was not a courtesan. Moreover he had a curiously virginal air as if he were not yet married, which he should have been long before this. He was taller than most Egyptian men and held his head with an almost womanly pride.

I determined to satisfy my curiosity and striding over to him demanded to know who he was. He was haughty and sulky, and I had some difficulty in extracting the information I was bent upon; but he no doubt realized that I would cuff him soundly if he refused to speak, and he finally, and by no means respectfully, informed me that he was the only child of a wealthy widow, whom I had known some years ago and who was now an invalid. And that he was twenty years old.

'Twenty!' I exclaimed. 'And unmarried! What is your mother thinking of?'

'My mother does not wish to part from me, nor do I wish to leave her,' he replied curtly.

'But a daughter-in-law would be far more useful to her — and more companionable — than a boy. And she must have granddaughters to inherit her property. Boys cannot inherit, as you well know.'

Again that detestable satiric expression crossed his face and he had the insolence to look me straight in the eye as he said coolly: 'All that may be changed one of these days, you know.'

I had a flash of memory and advanced upon him threateningly. 'Ha!' I cried. 'I have heard rumors of clubs where men meet and talk about equal rights. Equal rights! Man's place is the home. I shall instruct the police to root out these secret meeting places and suppress them.'

He shrugged. 'Very likely they will succeed. And beat us, no doubt. But — well — let them do their worst. And you. It won't matter in the end. There aren't many of us now; most of the men of Egypt are miserable parasites, fit for nothing but to be husbands of tyrannical females. But there are a few of us who are different, and we think our brains are as good as yours if not better. And in the next generation there will be many more.'

'You are nothing but a spoilt brat!' I thundered. 'What you need is a good spanking. I shall call upon your mother myself and see that she marries you at once.'

'Try it.' And turning on his heel without ceremony he walked off with the stride of a woman. I walked slowly to my office, somewhat disturbed. This was a type of young man new to me. I could not see him going to bed with the baby to keep it warm, nor titivating himself before the mirror, nor practising all the silly little arts of his sex to wheedle money out of his wife to spend in the bazars. Were there many like him? I had received the impression that although he had found an impudent pleasure in defying me, he had not told me half. Deceitful hussies. Liars. You never know where you are with the best of them. As for *him* the thing to do was to marry him to a fine healthy girl who would present him with ten daughters. That would take the starch out of him.

But I found more men in my office to transact important business, and forgot him. Nor did I remember to call on his mother, nor to instruct the police, for other ships came in, and more rumors of war, although nothing came of them in the end. When he crossed my mind he seemed too unimportant for consideration by busy women. Let him and his silly friends amuse themselves with their 'clubs.' Who cared? *Men.*

And so in my ancient arrogance I disdained that first faint warning note of revolt in the subordinate sex. In succeeding generations it sounded more stridently, and not only in Egypt but in all the women's states. The time came when we were awake to the danger and fought those determined men bitterly, but in the end we were compelled to grant them equal rights. We became reconciled. As a matter of fact we were happier as men grew in both mental and physical stature and we were forced to respect and treat them as equals. We wondered if our ancestresses hadn't found it rather boring to have no companionship save with members of their own sex.

That period of complete equality was the happiest in the history of either sex.

But alas, one who has been the underdog is never satisfied with mere equality. By imperceptible degrees those men increased in numbers, in power, became mighty on the battlefield, grabbed the best positions in the state, until that long blissful period of equality was over and man became the dominant, woman the subordinate sex. Then — after centuries of submission to the tyrannical male, women grew as restive, as resentful, as aspiring and ambitious, as those men of ancient times. Slowly but surely the new revolution spread over the more enlightened countries.

2

We are now in the first stage of sex equality, but the first only. The winning of the franchise was the initial step, little more. Man still bestrides the world like a colossus. But let us see how firm his foundations are today.

If men had given women the franchise when they first asked for it, no doubt it would have gone the way of all new toys when the novelty wore off, and women in the mass would have been totally uninterested. But man's stubbornness and injustice roused the fighting spirit in increasing thousands and the grim unyielding struggle began.

Let us confine ourselves to the United States where the movement was initiated.

Between thirty and forty years ago the self-supporting women were authors and other artists, actresses, opera singers, newspaperwomen, nurses, a few doctors, government clerks, a limited number of typists, schoolteachers, boarding-house-keepers, dressmakers, sewing-women who went out by the day, shop girls, servants. Exclusive of the last, they numbered something like four thousand.

In 1920 the census revealed there were 8,500,000 employed women in the United States. In 1930, 10,-752,116. The Depression accounted for the slow *advance*, but it is a fact well known that thousands of servants had been dismissed, firms great and small either retrenched or closed down, many typists and girls otherwise employed in offices and industries lost their jobs. And as for the women who had invaded the business world independently and were successfully competing with men, they had a hard struggle and many went under.

But bad times pass. In due course all of these women and more will be at work again, and there is little doubt that in another five years their numbers will have scaled a far higher peak than that of 1930. In the business and professional world particularly they will assert their equality in increasing numbers, and the time will come when Big Business Women, women eminent in science and the professions, will cease to be phenomena. Everywhere one sees exclusive shops run by women, and their beauty salons flourished all through the Depression.

Significant as is the upward sweep of their present condition, even more so is the immense activity of women in public organizations. The old Browning Clubs (the original Highbrows!) and other ladylike gatherings have given place to great mobilizations like the National League of Women Voters, numbering many thousands, for it is composed of thirty-six affiliated State Leagues and six hundred local leagues; the National Federation of Women's Clubs, intellectual women deeply interested in current history; the International Federation of Business and Professional Women's Clubs, already numbering a hundred thousand and rapidly increasing, whose activities and accomplishment would appal men if they took a little time off to investigate and ponder. The D.A.R.'s may become a political power.

The National Women's Party is out to fight for a constitutional amendment guaranteeing equal rights to men and women in all arenas, to say nothing of their other formidable activities. The National League of American Penwomen, composed of professional women in all the arts from writing to architecture, with 2459 members, and branches in all important cities, is concerned with cultural development. It abjures politics, but its members vote more intelligently and conscientiously than many groups of men we could mention, and its mass influence is very great.

In 1936 the National League of Women Voters held more than ten thousand meetings in thirty-six states and approximately six hundred communities. The State Leagues worked on three hundred and ninety-six measures before the legislatures, of which one hundred and fifty-six were passed. With the close of the 1937 California Legislature all major bills supported by the League were passed and all bills opposed by the League defeated. One of those bills, initiated by the League, brought a minor department of the state into a major position in state government. All the Leagues were active in supporting nine federal measures in the second session of the Seventy-Fourth Congress. Here are a few of the vital problems to which they give unremitting attention: Government and Economic Welfare; Government and its Operations; Government and Foreign Policy; Government and Child Welfare; Government and Education; Government and Legal Status of Women. What they have already accomplished would fill another article. But what they are out for above all is complete equality in all respects, not merely permission to go to the polls; and let no one doubt the outcome.

Aside from these powerful organizations, of which I have mentioned but the most important, there is probably not a town in the United States that has not only its cultural clubs, but forums devoted to the study of politics, and civic and governmental questions of immediate import. Women have already elbowed their way into Congress, state legislatures, civic jobs, and we have all heard of one or two governors and mayors.

Two or three women elevated to high places have made complete fools of themselves, and, perhaps, momentarily darkened the prospects of women in general. But let the world pause and reflect upon the thousands of public men past and present who have made fools of *them*selves. And as for private life — ask any married woman how often her husband seems to her ridiculous and inadequate. But no one except fanatical idealists indulges in the hope of remaking human nature.

And now San Francisco is to have a Woman's Chamber of Commerce.

Mr. Uzzell and Mr. Le Roy, in a magazine article, lamented that 'women buy eighty per cent of the consumer's goods; are the chief beneficiaries of most estates; receive eighty per cent of the benefits of life insurance; about forty per cent of all railroad corporations; some forty per cent of all real estate. Ninety per cent of American spending is controlled by women. They own seventy-five per cent of the Nation's wealth, seventy-five per cent of all suburban homes, as well as forty per cent of all real estate. . . . The male today is without his prophets, his laureates. . . . After a century-long campaign for the "rights of women" we find victory more than won. Woman has effectively demonstrated that she can equal his feats of physical endurance in swimming and in certain sports, can wear his clothes, invade his barber shop, smoke his pipe, and swear. Still she is not content.'

The conservative *New York Times* confessed itself aghast at an advertisement sent in by 'Woman's Inventions in America Incorporated,' and commented: 'They talk boldly about women deciding what the Nation should eat and wear, where and how it should live, what is good for it and what is not. America isn't a democracy, it is a matriarchy!'

Writes Isaac Marcosson, *savant* of American reporters: 'It may startle the atavistic males to learn that women today are beneficiaries of 80 per cent of the nation's $104,500,000,000 outstanding life insurance, on which $2,000,000,000 is being paid out every year. Any insurance company will tell you that women are outliving the men. The private wealth of the nation is only $280,000,000,000, and women already own enough of that to make the he-Titans tremble. But the women don't know it.'

(Oh, don't they, Mr. Marcosson?)

'In 1934 Mrs. Catherine Curtis went on a radio program and talked once a week on "Women and Money."... Every time she talked she asked the women of the radio audience if they would like to see organized a group known as "Women Investors in America," which would study finance, economics, and legislation affecting women's investments. Shoals of letters came in approving the plan, with the result that Women Investors in America, which now has forty thousand members, was incorporated in May,

1935. It has become the forum of petticoat finance. . . .
The women's dollar cavalcade pushes on with banners
flying stock and board certificates and realty deeds.
Are we headed for a financial matriarchy? Will the
father of tomorrow plaintively ask, "Did I rear my
boy to work for a woman?" '

None of these semi-jocular, semi-grieving gentlemen
has fathomed the true meaning of the portent. No
doubt they regard it as a nuisance, but as sporadic as
strikes. It will be some time before they realize that
the long era of male dominance is approaching its
end, and that women are striding, millions strong,
along the road to complete equality.

And are women dominated personally by men as of
yore? As if in answer to Otto Weininger's silly asser-
tion that women are wholly sensual and have no
character apart from their relation to men, a jury in
Newark, New Jersey, in 1936, composed entirely of
women, brought in a verdict of guilty against a fascinating and eloquent young rascal, who had been so
sure of his blandishments that he had demanded a
jury of the once weaker sex.

Doctor C. J. Jung, who has psychoanalyzed thousands of women, is more wide-awake and therefore
more pessimistic. 'There used to be societies for the
protection of young girls,' says he. 'They are no
longer necessary. Women can take care of themselves,
and the societies could do well to reverse their aims
and set out to protect young men from girls. . . . The
women patients who come to me now with their
problems are a different type from the ones of a past

generation. No longer are girls timid or shrinking. They have changed places with the men. Women have become the Don Juans.'

Judge Marshall F. McComb, of the Los Angeles Court of Appeals, is equally disillusioned. Holding that 'the individuality of the female sex has been materially advanced by the advent of the radio and motion pictures and the wide dissemination of information regarding the sexes,' he reversed a $10,000 judgment awarded to an eighteen-year-old girl, who asserted she had been 'betrayed.'

And what of the tremendous mass movement in 1936 in the State of Washington, when thousands of women of all classes and from all over the state invaded Seattle, crowding its streets and overflowing its great auditorium, for the purpose of 'ridding our state of the racketeering monster which has been fostered by machine politicians, threatening the ruin of helpless industries and individuals?' The objects of their particular wrath were the Governor of the state, and the Mayor of Seattle — who wrung his hands and cried: 'Don't let them make a fool of me! What have I ever done to be held up to scorn and contumely?' I don't pretend to know the right or wrong of the case. The only point worth considering is that when the women arose in their might a Johnstown flood would have been more welcome.

Nor are the women of far-away Poland to be despised. Here is a cable from Bialystok dated June 18, 1937: 'Threateningly swinging umbrellas and clubs, five hundred wives and daughters today abruptly forced an end to a five-week strike of seven hundred workmen who had refused to accept arbitration proposals. The men had turned down the management's offer to grant them half of their demands when their women folk appeared on the scene and threatened to beat their hold-out husbands and fathers.

'The agreement was signed immediately and the men returned to their jobs.'

Bernarr MacFadden called attention in one of his editorials to the fact that in Phoenix, Arizona, five hundred women had banded together with the view to attacking corrupt office-holders, and hoped their example would be followed throughout the country. His hope will be fulfilled, no doubt, for in many states similar organizations are working openly or secretly against intolerable conditions, and will make a public demonstration when the time is ripe.

There are many other signal posts dotting the landscape. Men are suing for alimony, patronizing beauty parlors in the hope of fascinating foolish middle-aged women with a full purse. But even the most manly of their sex — and they still are in the majority — have never even guessed that their shaven faces and women's plank-like figures are symptoms of the unconscious urge of the sexes toward equality.

Nevertheless... Mr. Harry Hansen, in reviewing Marjorie Hillis' novel 'Orchids in Your Budget,' began with the remark: 'One of our national scandals that gets far too little attention is the decline of the married man in prestige and influence,' and went on to lament that the author was unkind and possibly unjust to the mere husbands of her dominant females. He refers to 'the extraordinary collection of weak-kneed males with which Miss Hillis encumbers her resourceful Amazons. Although a few men are spoken of with respect, many of them seem to be mere saps, letting their wives do all sorts of queer things, etc. . . . If he (the husband) has the faintest hint of a flair for cooking, fan it like a dying flame; it may be a tremendous asset in entertaining. If he really likes it you are made as a hostess. . . . Throughout the book runs a complete disregard of the capacities of the male as a financial prop. If he works hard at his job, he is just a drone with no parlor conversation. . . . Heroism, so far as this book is concerned, is a feminine quality. It's the woman who says: "What if we do lose our money? *I'll* work." . . . They (the men) are sad descendants of the Puritan Fathers. Those old-timers, at least, would not have trailed behind their women with a tray of canapés. Nor would the Puritan women, whose capacity for work was some shades better than those of the orchidaceous Mrs. X, Mrs. Y, and Mrs. Z, have tolerated such parasitic mates.'

All of which is faintly reminiscent of the fifth century B.C.

Another woman has written: 'A girl's upbringing today differs from that of her grandmother as much in independence of attitude as in scholastic subject matter. Her viewpoint and her willingness — nay eagerness — to try new things rival that of her brothers.'

Very different from the ultra-feminine minxes of

yesteryear, and if they sometimes abuse their freedom they are merely following the age-old male standards.

And how about other standards, to come back to the title of this article? It has been sufficiently demonstrated that, with the sole exception of a rudimentary difference in sex, women are no more congenital in any respect than men. You might as well talk about born athletes or born scholars. The tendency, yes; but one that is extinguished or developed by conditions. But tendencies *plus* conditions ever-growing, ever-developing both under blind forces and cunning manipulation, work inexorably toward the alternating eras of male and female dominance. As to lying: With the millions of women who are now out in the business world, or members of serious organizations for the betterment of mankind, and their own government in particular, it may safely be assumed that lying has gone out with 'trains' for street wear, curves, hat pins, 'airs,' and clumsy make-up. Of course we still have a fine quota of fools and parasites, but even they will feel the force of example in time. Fashion is fashion.

This article nor a hundred like it will wake men up. Male arrogance is still too strong. But if it did they would be helpless. The tide is in full spate. No mortal hand can turn it back.

It is amusing to think of this revolution going on almost out of sight but gathering strength and momentum with every crowded year, while men grow excited over the menaces of fascism, communism, the proletariat, this demagogue and that, strikes, and what not.

Plato, Christ, Kant, approved of that equality which is once more under way. Nature certainly had it in mind when she planted male hormones in women and female hormones in men. And it is to be hoped that when women have achieved it, in its fullest sense, they will be content, and not push on toward dominance. Either extreme is fatal to happiness, which can be found in its full perfection only when neither sex has cause to despise the other.

Nor is there any reason to believe that Woman Dominant would do any better than man has done with the world as we know it through the pages of history. Man and Woman are merely human nature under two different labels. Two horns on the same old cow.

CHAPTER II
WHY WOMEN CAN'T
BE GENTLEMEN

EVEN in these days when so many dull novels are being written about the proletariat, and intellectuals and sophisticates have fallen over one another in their haste to climb on the bandwagon, about the most stinging epithet that may be applied to a man is 'not a gentleman.' Tradition dies hard. It is doubtful if even communists — outside of Russia — who profess such scorn of the 'bourgeoisie,' would relish being called cads or bounders.

Undoubtedly the word gentleman was first applied, in our language at least, to Englishmen of inherited property — nobility and landed gentry; in other words to those fortunate persons who were not obliged to work for their living. During the nineties I spent several months in the villages of England, avoiding the inns and living with the natives when they could be persuaded to give me room and board. I suffered acute discomfort, but at that time I intended to live in England and wanted to understand it from the roots up. I remember that my Americanism was somewhat startled to hear them refer to 'the gentleman class' and as naturally as they would have spoken of thoroughbred horses. Coming from a land where 'I guess I am as good as you are' might be called a national slogan, I wondered at first that people so evidently self-respecting and independent could make such a tacit admission without loss of pride. But to those good people it was one of the laws of life and it had never occurred to them to dispute nor resent it. Scions of great families might be boorish or brutal, card sharps or swindlers. Never mind. Class was class. If a man was born a gentleman so he remained until the end of his days, even if hastily shipped abroad by his family to become a remittance man on some palm-lined shore.

Ballard Smith, when living in London as head of the *New York World* news bureau, told me that his secretary, a refined and educated young man, once said to him sadly: 'Oh, Mr. Smith, you don't know what it means in England not to have been born a gentleman.' He might have added that the only hope the lowly-born had of rising out of his class and sitting at table with dukes was to possess the genius for making money in vast quantities and allying himself with the nobility by marriage. Many an ancient house has been saved by such an alliance, and dukes are notoriously democratic when it suits their purpose. Far more so than villagers and servants. To them those intruders would never be included in the 'gentleman class.'

Not to be unfair to the English, it must be admitted

that long before the levelling War they extended a generous hospitality to men and women of inferior birth who had distinguished themselves in any one of the arts, and, all conceded, had formed an aristocracy of their own. This was by no means the case with all continental Society groups in the days when they were ruled by aristocrats.

In the United States the term gentleman has a wider interpretation, possibly because men of lineage are scarce. A man may have been born in a pigsty, but if he manages to get a good education, and nature has given him adaptability and aspiration, he is accepted without argument. To be a gentleman in the United States of America it is enough to have impeccable manners and grammar, a high standard of honor, self-respect without bumptiousness, kindness, and tact. On the other hand a man may be enjoying wealth in the third generation, but if his manners and personality are offensive we do not hesitate to characterize him as 'not a gentleman,' and see as little of him as possible.

With us, interesting minds and inoffensive manners are found in all classes, even among those who make no attempt to raise themselves to the higher social brackets. I once went out to lunch with a plumber. A man in San Francisco, whose talents had lifted him high above his humble beginnings, told me that he suffered a good deal from a brother-in-law, a master plumber, an intelligent man but who professed a violent scorn and even hatred of 'Society,' and was convinced that all members of it were fools, parasites, idlers, tricksters, and should be exterminated by law. He was not a Marxian, for he had no quarrel with men who were clever enough to pile up fortunes; their only offence lay in permitting their wives and daughters to make fools of them. So far he had contemptuously refused to meet any of his relative's new friends, and derided him as a snob and a climber.

If a meeting could be arranged without exciting this man's suspicions would I mind 'being nice' to him, and perhaps convince him of error? Always on the alert for a new experience, I consented readily. I met the plumber, and we got along admirably. He invited me to lunch at 'The Market,' a favorite resort of business men at that hour. I found his table manners irreproachable and his conversation excellent. We talked politics, plumbing, and books. But that was as far as I ever got with him, and, for that matter, I had avoided all mention of society or class. He insisted to his brother-in-law that I must be the exception — I wrote, didn't I, and received hard cash for my work? Of course that made me different — and would have no more of his friends. Perhaps he knew that despite his intelligence he never would become a gentleman even in the loosest American sense. He was rather uncouth in appearance, his manners were brusque, and he was hopelessly class-conscious. The last is fatal, and must have kept many a man and woman from achieving social success, unless irresistibly rich.

I never heard an English person of assured position make any reference to class. Their nearest approach was to say of some woman: 'She's — well — not quite a lady, don't you know?' Here in the United States where women are even more adaptable than men, their opportunities are equal and their success depends largely upon themselves. In less democratic days one met New York Society women whose manners were quite abominable, owing, it must have been, to a class-consciousness as itching as that of my plumber. But they were exceptional, and in Boston, Chicago, Indianapolis, Los Angeles (the 'old set'), Lexington, Kentucky, and San Francisco, which cover my experience of American society, I never met anything like them. They reminded me of certain middle-class women in London, whose wealth had elevated them socially and who had a dim idea that rudeness was an evidence of superiority.

But while American Society as a rule is too sure of itself or too good-natured for snobbishness, it is quite true that women born far beyond the sacred portals rarely find their way in except through the wealth and importance of their husbands. Sometimes not then if quite 'impossible.' But if, with increasing riches, they have travelled, overcome their early inadequacies, and kept their eyes and ears open, sooner or later they may have the exquisite pleasure of seeing their names on the Society pages of the newspapers. If Nature has endowed them with personality, initiative, and ambition, they may even become leaders. Never forget that the founder of one great New York family was an oyster dredger and another sold pelts on street corners. Hope for all.

But, oddly, while we are quick to denounce a man as 'no gentleman' we rarely or never hear the term 'no lady.' We seem to shy away from the word, and would faint with horror at hearing anyone called 'a perfect lady.' Not in these days. I fancy the term went out when young men of a certain class in the United States began speaking of his inamorata as 'me lady frien',' and the young ladies used the word as freely when alluding to one another. The comic weeklies took it up, and sounded the death knell of a fine old word of great traditions. Now, we will go no farther than to denounce a woman for not being a good sport.

That term, of course, includes the characteristics which go to the making of the American gentleman. There are plenty of women in Society, as out of it, who are mean and cattish and unreliable, but even when born in the purple they are severely criticized by those whose code of behavior is that of the highest type of American men, and who form the majority and hold social groups of all grades together. Therefore, when a man asked me why so few women had the instincts of gentlemen I was inspired to entitle this chapter with the question, in a briefer form, and dispose of it.

No doubt a certain percentage of men are irritated, early glamour having departed, by the indifference of their wives to the higher standards that have been forced upon men, and who fib, and scheme, and 'boss' in the effort to get the best of them. (A woman with a husband and two grown sons once told me that women had to lie awake nights thinking up resources to keep men from getting the best of *them*, but never mind.) Of course there are inferior women just as there are inferior men, or, to shift the viewpoint, the only kingdom of a certain breed of women is within the narrow confines of the home, and their natural aspiration is to rule it.

But — if those chafing males were able to evoke from the realm of shades a congress of Men of the Old School, say five thousand of them, confront them with an equal quota of modern husbands, and induce all to compare notes, they might be surprised to find that the number of ungentlemanly women had decreased in the ratio of a hundred to one.

When men in ancient times were the subordinate sex and were forced to resort to every mean device to get the best — occasionally — of their female tyrants, they had neither time nor aspiration for those higher standards of conduct upon which dominant woman prided herself. Inferior in ethics as in stature, they lied and schemed and 'managed.' I shouldn't be surprised if they had hysterics.

And so it was with women for many centuries. Men were household tyrants — old novels are full of them; also, 'conflict' between the old and the new generation was a fertile subject in fiction when the world was still a slave to tradition.

Unquestionably the long struggle of women for the franchise, their open rebellion against subjection to men, awoke women in general, sharpened their wits, poured steel into the waiting moulds of their characters, started a revolution both mental and psychic. Impossible for those pioneers, at least, to take a firm stand and keep it in the face of abuse, ridicule, constant thwartings, without developing self-respect; and self-respect is incompatible with ungentlemanly standards. Impossible for intelligent women in general to be uninfluenced.

That delectable writer, Harold Nicolson, in a recent book, 'Small Talk,' winds up his essay 'Defence of the American Man' with the following sentence: 'The American woman, on the other hand, is competitive, womanly, conceited, acquisitive, unimportant, tyrannical, and very very neat.'

Dear Mr. Nicolson, brilliant as you are, you *cannot* learn all there is to be known about American women in a few short months. 'Society' entertained you and your gifted wife in many cities which you visited briefly on your lecture tour, and we all know what the chatter at gatherings of that sort amounts to. How could you catch even a glimpse of the lives behind the vivacious, charmingly dressed 'fronts' of those women? Truth to tell, that sentence sounds as if lifted from some traveller's 'Impressions' of thirty years ago. It is quite true that in all social groups there are a number of women who think of nothing but dress, bridge, and gossip. But the majority today are deeply interested in politics, social welfare, and self-improvement. Even the Junior League girls devote certain days of every week to hospitals and clinics for poor children, and in San Francisco they have a 'home' in the suburbs for orphans and neglected children whom they feed, clothe, educate, and start in life when the time comes. No doubt every Junior League group in the United States has a similar charity.

And where did you get that idea, Mr. Nicolson, that the American man is driven to work like a dog by his tyrannical wife? The American Man's passion is BUSINESS. He eats, sleeps, drinks, thinks business. It is the god of his idolatry. Paris never loved Helen, nor Pericles Aspasia as he loves the great game of making money, piling up riches, getting ahead of the other fellow. His wife is lucky if she can get any table conversation out of him, and although generous (unless he is one of the stingy ones, of which we have quite a number), and taking pride in the glittering effect of his hard-earned dollars on his wife's back, when he has time to think about it, he would work just as hard for those dollars if he were a bachelor — as we have abundant evidence, even among the young unmarried men. Unless a politician by trade, his only interest in politics is their effect on BUSINESS, and never has he been so excited over them as during the Franklin Delano Roosevelt administration. Spend three years with us, Mr. Nicolson. We'd love to have you.

Unconsciously, and long before the granting of the franchise, the pervasion of the new idea was absorbed by young women who gave no thought to the vote but saw no reason why their outdoor life should not be as free as that of their brothers, and invaded the unprofessional world of sport. All young women and girls who could afford it, and were not hopelessly 'feminine,' spent a part of the day riding (astride), swimming, playing tennis or golf, and, later, racing about the country in sport cars. For the first time they associated with men as comrades, instead of sitting at home hoping that some man would call, practicing sentimental songs, or wondering wistfully how many 'beaux' would ask them to dance at the next party. And I shouldn't wonder if some of them did the proposing. Sport marked the true beginning of sex equality, in this country at least, and as the girls had more time for practice they were often more than a match for the sons of disapproving fathers. 'When I was a young man, etc.' And without becoming de-feminized these girls, quite naturally, were good sports in every sense of the word. In due course the whole standard of Society was elevated.

Another word in regard to the influence of sport on the young. It may have been noticed that for a good many years now all the silly, sentimental, and impossibly romantic novels have been written for the middle-middle and lower-middle class, whose lives are drab and who still try to believe in fairy tales. Young people in the upper brackets have become intensely matter-of-fact. After overhearing a conversation on a train between two of them, evidently strongly attracted, but whose minds at the moment appeared to be concentrated on the last polo match, I wondered what form his words would take when he proposed to her. 'What do you say if we hitch-up?' was my conclusion. It may not always be as bad as that, but impossible that any one of these young persons, no matter how much in love (that is, race-victims during the mating years) would indulge in the impassioned declarations of yore.

But that is a digression, although not wholly beside the point. In the previous chapter I called attention to the fact that there are now millions of women in the United States who are out in the world earning their living on equal terms with men in business and the professions, thousands more who are active members of great organizations that demand the highest order of intelligence, for they are designed for the elevation not only of women but of the world in general; and with an influence in politics and economics that no sensible man ignores. Of equal energy and portent are the thousands of women's clubs in the smaller cities and towns.

Now, no one will deny that many men are liars, but the fact remains that civilization would disintegrate into chaos unless in business, in the professions, even in politics, a man's word was 'as good as his bond.' A high code of honor is forced upon men if only because self-interest demands it. Men must pull together in whatever field they choose to till, and the crooked, the unreliable, among them are squeezed out as a hindrance and a nuisance.

Many men, it is true, are honorable by long tradition, their motives far more elevated than those inspired merely by self-interest, and high-minded young men are turned out of our colleges by the thousands every year. Even when disillusioned by life or struggling for place in the maelstrom of the business world they automatically cling to their standards. The point is that the standards are imperative.

It can hardly be disputed that women must adopt the same standards if they would compete on equal terms with men, or make an outstanding success of those great organizations that may breed a race of superwomen. To say nothing of college women, into whom precisely the same code of honor is instilled as in the case of their brothers, no body of women great or small can pull together in harness or accomplish anything at all unless reasonably truthful, reliable, well-mannered, considerate and kind, no matter what their inflexibility of purpose.

Very well, then, women cannot practise the more elevated attributes of our poor human nature (nothing to brag about at best) without developing all the 'instincts' of a gentleman, any more than Helen Wills could cheat at tennis, or I, for instance, could brag that I had sold a hundred thousand copies of a book when the presses had cooled off at ten thousand.

There are millions and millions of women today — and it is time men digested this fact — whose 'instincts' are quite as gentlemanly as those of man at his best. The word 'instincts' is a misnomer, by the way. Do not small children steal as naturally as puppies (who would lie also if they could talk), until they are remade at the end of a switch? Most of our good instincts are pounded into us during our formative years. The bad instincts we are born with are inherited memories from our remotest ancestors who were also formed by conditions.

Personally, I have met with more meanness, spite, petty jealousy, from men than from any member of my own sex — or at least with few exceptions. I fancy that any woman who puts herself before the public and achieves any measure of success, has the same experience. Women take pride in the success of other women, but men seem to resent it as a personal insult. When I was very young I said wonderingly to John Habberton, 'Why, men are as spiteful as women.' His reply was: 'My dear child, spite is a human not a sex quality.' Certainly it is not a gentlemanly one. Oddly enough, however, the only men I have known who were spiteful, mean, and petty were knights of the pen in one way or another. I should like to hear the experiences of women painters, sculptors, musicians, to say nothing of actresses and prima donnas.

CHAPTER III

WHY DO WOMEN

HATE ONE ANOTHER?

THE impressions one receives in one's plastic years are strong and deep, but fortunately not ineradicable. Two of mine, however, are vivid in memory.

My mother, although devoted to her husband, was high-strung and flared up on the slightest provocation; my stepfather was stubborn, superior, and provoking. A child takes no note of other households, and I grew up in the firm belief that all married couples quarrelled incessantly and there was no such thing as happiness in the married state. This affected me so profoundly that I flatly refused to quarrel with my own husband, which sometimes caused him acute annoyance. I also observed that two of my sisters-in-law, who were little younger than my mother, took their husbands philosophically and were reasonably happy. Nevertheless, that early impression affected my work for a number of years, for the subconscious is a silent partner of obtrusive habits.

The second impression lasted longer and for multiple reasons, some of them absurd, others a part of the pattern of that unenlightened era.

In these days women have innumerable things to talk about; the interests of the intelligent at least are as varied as those of men, in some cases more so. But in that far-off time of the sixties and seventies it would seem that their only subjects of conversation were dress, children, servants, and gossip. Above all, gossip. There were no women's clubs for self-improvement nor for the improvement of the sex in general. Bridge was unborn. They did not even play Poker nor Whist. The only women of this class who 'worked for their living' were schoolteachers and boarding-house-keepers — plenty of the latter, in San Francisco at least, for husbands were always blowing out their brains after a prolonged debauch on the stock market. Teachers may have discussed books when they met; 'reduced ladies' who took boarders had little time to talk about anything. But for women of leisure gossip was the main resource.

I remember a large front bedroom where my mother received her friends, and where they would sit for hours gossiping, or, to put it more precisely, tearing reputations to pieces. My mother was a beauty, and diplomacy being no part of her mental constitution, had made enemies of other women, who, like herself, had no interest in anything but their personal affairs. She was a good hater and so were her friends. Friends. Perhaps. She fell out with them now and then and reviled them to her unsympathetic husband. Doubtless they relieved their own minds in a similar manner.

At school I made friends, but more rivals, for I was determined to be first or die, and so were others. Bitter rivalries and hates.

During my married years when life was more tranquil — and dull — I rarely heard women discuss anything but personalities, a fashionable novel, or some actress who was 'the rage.' They may have been dependent for happiness upon their husbands, but they took no interest in business or the professions, and lived their days in a small world of their own. That they lived under male domination troubled them not at all, unless, to be sure, the husband was subject to delirium tremens, or too utterly 'incompatible,' when they divorced him. But not often. Divorce left a social stigma on the woman, and she preferred to accept the rôle of the unhappy, complaining, or embittered wife. The husbands consoled themselves elsewhere, the wives met in front bedrooms, and, when too well bred to discuss their erring mates, found compensation in scandalmongering; which did nothing to elevate their minds nor strengthen their characters.

It was an unfortunate period for women, and, despite the fact that strong souls here and there were giving voice to resentment at male domination, startling the world with their loud demands for political equality, the sex in general may be said to have touched bottom.

And more particularly in the United States. In Britain and France women of the upper class took an interest in politics and a few *salons* were famous; in

France, women of the lower bourgeoisie were their husbands' partners in business. But American women, outside the narrow confines of Washington, D.C., knew nothing of politics and were excluded from business. And husbands, as a rule, were easygoing, many spoilt their wives even when they neglected them. For a man to make a companion of his wife was almost unheard of.

We all know the names of the great women who founded the political revolution of their sex, but who was the unsung benefactress in whose aspiring mind was born the idea of the Literary Club? Probably someone in New England, our intellectual Alma Mater. At all events there came a time when those clubs were springing up all over the land, and women by the hundreds were discussing something besides dress, children, servants, and gossip. Their gropings were feeble at first, and they were the subject of much good-natured ridicule, but they had begun definitely to climb up from the pit of inconsequence.

Then came the famous Browning Clubs. More ridicule, but marking another shakeup of their intellectual particles.

Now it stands to reason that when women began to respect their own minds and the minds of others of their sex associated with them in a common interest — self-improvement — they had taken a long swing upward and personalities had ceased to be the major interest of their leisure hours. If there were still rivalries and jealousies they were on a higher plane, and the effect was stimulating, not debasing.

Another bond was formed between women when they developed an interest in cards. At first it was the gentle Casino and Five Hundred, rarely Whist or Poker. But in due course all of these were superseded by the now universal Bridge.

Cards did more to draw women together than even the Literary Club, which met only once or twice a month. Groups met several times a week for their absorbing game, and when Bridge became prevalent, a game that demanded mental concentration and self-control, and quickened the intellect, women, particularly those past their first youth, and dependent upon one another for enlivening an otherwise dull existence, formed deep and abiding friendships in which the old petty jealousies and hatreds could find no corner for resurgence.

If one studies the history of nations, including current history, it must strike the most uninvestigating mind that hate has been rampant in the world since Cain murdered Abel; and that its forces for the most part have been concentrated in the minds of men. Many of those hates have altered the course of history. Hatred has poisoned religions, politics, precipitated wars, ruined careers, played a large part in crime. Which only goes to prove that hate, like envy, spite, vanity, petty jealousies, and a tendency to hysteria, are not sex failings at all but manifestations of human nature in the general. Women would not be human if they were incapable of hate, and doubtless many women in public life would like to stick a knife into rivals who pass or thwart them, but the millions who have lifted themselves to a plane where their minds have developed manifold interests, no longer hate other women on general principles.

Far be it from me to contend there are not other millions who are still absorbed in their own little worlds to the exclusion of all else. Who read nothing but the sensational items in the newspapers and second-rate novels, listen to idiotic radio 'entertainments,' whose intimacies at the Bridge table — if they have brains enough to play Bridge — breed nervous irritation that explodes in bickering or serious quarrels. Who may hate other women in their small circle that dress better, have larger incomes, more indulgent husbands, receive more attention from men, or who are smart enough to seize the reins of leadership.

There is not much to be said for the average of intelligence in either sex. When young men in the United States were being drafted for the World War it was discovered that their mental average was thirteen and a half years.

No such test has yet been applied to women, but one has only to listen to those radio programs between 9 A.M. and 5 P.M. designed for female morons. I am recommending a hideous ordeal, but one both salutary and chastening for those of us who have become prematurely enthusiastic over the fact that increasing millions of our women are now the equals of first-rate men in initiative, intelligence, accomplishment, and constructive effort. The net impression will be that there are many millions more who revel in mental fodder that would be scorned by a bright boy of sixteen.

43

The only consolation is to be found in listening to some of the radio programs concocted for men.

It is rather appalling to consider that the majority of these women are the wives and mothers of the nation; they are not on relief because in their youthful prettiness and charm they appealed to men with a weak spot in their superior brains. Therefore, it is plain to be seen why so many American men have a low estimate of women in general. Excluding men gifted in one or other of the arts and who have an extra supply of female hormones that gives them a broader understanding of the sex and inclines them to a stronger type of woman, it is small wonder that men still regard women as the inferior sex. A man's wife may be faithful and devoted, a good housekeeper and mother; but all that he takes for granted and judges her mentally — and through her all women save the famous exceptions — by her conversational gabble and her relations with the women of her intimate circle. Undoubtedly as a wife he prefers her to 'one of those women who do things,' and loves her the more — tepidly — for the sense of masculine superiority she fosters, but he despises her, and, as a natural corollary, her entire sex.

Well, unless physiological morons, even these women sometimes grow up. More and more of them in an era when it is becoming the fashion to know a little of everything. And mentally, the life of a woman who has married young (unless she is one of Art's chosen), does not begin until her children spend their days at school. What latent intelligence she may have

44

is then free to develop, even if she has to do her own work, for electricity does most of it for her. Many women are surprised to find they have a submerged personality only too eager to come into its own. These women are quick to make a new life for themselves. They join an important club and become deeply interested in public service. They find a job, or, if they can raise the capital, enter the business world independently.

If confirmed in domesticity, they read the important books, take up some study, attend morning lectures, where the news of the world is lucidly interpreted, and cultivate other women of similar tastes. Whether they become the companion and friend of their husbands depends a good deal upon the husbands. American men are such gluttons for work, especially when young, that although devoted and faithful, they have, after an engrossing day in the office, law courts, or whatever, little energy left for the home. They fall asleep before dinner and are hibernating at nine o'clock. A wife's companionship to them is a beautiful abstraction. If American women have learned to be more independent of men than any women in the world, the blame should not be laid upon either but upon the age they live in. After the mating season has run its initial course American women are literally forced to take refuge in the society of one another. The vast majority of the more intelligent are well fitted to be the companions of men and would welcome the ideal relationship if it could be achieved. But in this modern economic world, that desideratum, except in rare cases, is impossible, and the result will be a solidarity of women, too experienced to quarrel and hate one another, that will increasingly threaten the supremacy of the male, although he is still too blind or too arrogant to suspect it.

O. O. McIntyre, in one of his columns, gave an interesting picture of 'Ladies Who Live Alone.' 'Spinsters by choice, who make their way in the world quietly, efficiently, and ask no odds of man. They are particularly noticeable in the sedate tea rooms at the dinner hour. Many are high-salaried secretaries — in some instances garnering fifteen thousand dollars a year. Then there are fashion designers, the owners of specialty shops, free-lance writers, and those skilled in that comparatively new and highly geared outergate post known as receptionist. Almost invariably in dining they imbibe but one cocktail slowly, meditatively, and puff one cigarette daintily with coffee. They express a distinct neatness in dress that sets them apart. And their dignity repels the most audacious flirt. Most of them are girls left young to fend for themselves. Some have little apartments on the fringe of the business district. Some occupy rooms in the great midtown hotels. They are careerists who symbolize compellingly the new emancipation of women.'

More solidarity. And is it conceivable that these women hate one another? Odd, also, they should be overlooked by married men when summing up women in general.

But to return to the domestic problem. One night at a dinner when the subject of husbands was under discussion, a young man asked me: 'What in your opinion *is* the ideal husband?' I cast about hastily in my mind and then replied: 'Why — no husband at all.'

Of course there was a general laugh, but it had occurred to me that I had never envied any woman her husband (as a husband) and never at any time would have exchanged my freedom for 'the best man that ever lived,' whatever that may mean. For some years after my husband died I used to day-dream romantically about the perfect mate, until I reluctantly came to the conclusion that no such being existed, on this planet at least, and that I should not know what to do with him if he had. Nor could I give these young people a list of the deceased ideal's virtues. Always nebulous, he had receded into the ether of which he had been born.

Someone else asked me if it were not true that I liked men better than women, and if so why I had no use for them as husbands. Well — it is one thing to enjoy a man's society for an hour or two now and then, and another to annex him permanently. Men, of course (some men), are more companionable to any intelligent woman than the most admired and respected of her own sex, but that has always seemed to me a good reason for not marrying them.

Not that I am answering for women in general. I think it tragic that in the stress of modern life men are unable to develop an ideal mental relationship with their wives. What poor mortals yearn for above all things is happiness; but not to be obtained without a similarity of tastes, interests, aspirations — *and* the leisure wherein to discover and cultivate them. Men and women, fitted to be the perfect companions, meet and marry. The man is haunted by vague regrets. The woman lives on hope. The exceptions are the most enviable of mortals — until the jealous gods can stand it no longer and play them some scurvy trick.

I mentioned on this same occasion that I had been asked to write an article on why women hated one another. This was a very friendly crowd of young moderns (the men were at least half-awake, one or two wholly so), and they laughed again. It was the women who answered. 'How like a man!' 'What nonsense!' 'Well — I might hate a woman who took my husband from me, but as for *all* my friends, they are splendid.' Indeed, one of the young women was accused of caring more for her friends than for her husband; she insisted upon living in San Francisco, and as her husband's business was in Seattle, she saw him only at week-ends. This was not true, of course. She is merely determined to have it both ways.

What did I think? Did *I* hate women? I had always been very polite and nice — but, well, one never knew.

I have never been much of an introvert, having passed the greater part of my life in creating characters — that is to say, adapting them from real life — or in resurrecting the great dead and trying to make them and their historic past live again: a far more fascinating pastime than sitting down and probing the tortuosities of one's ego. But in all my personal relationships I could not recall personal hate for any man or woman; although I had heartily disliked some of both sexes, felt a profound contempt for others, and resented injustice and the meannesses bred by envy and spite — of men not of women — that I had encountered so often in my career. But hatred was a compliment I had reserved for another breed.

Who are they? Well, certain men who have thrust themselves too far forward in public life. I have hated — do hate — certain notorious men so violently that were I only a witch I would blast them out of life without a scruple. If I don't go out and shoot them it is not because I fear the exacting of an eye for an eye, for I am sure some clever lawyer would get me off (to say nothing of a grateful public), but because there are no private baths in jails, and I am too unused to restraint to suffer even a week of it with equanimity. I have always envied Rider Haggard's She, who could hurl a bolt of lightning from her finger-tips and shrivel a man to one long cinder. I cherish the hope that when I am a discarnate spirit this power will be mine; so, if after my exit, certain obnoxious demagogues, who, for their own selfish ends, have been racketeering to the discomfort of a helpless public, drop in their tracks, one right after another, you will know what has happened.

(ALSO CROONERS)

CHAPTER IV

BORED ON

HER STAR

AN ADMIRAL of the United States Navy who had sailed the seven seas once told me that the inhabitants of the remotest isles, who had never seen a white man before his ship anchored off shore, all indulged in some form of intoxication — and in gambling. The really remarkable part of it to me was that although they found it easy enough to concoct an intoxicating brew out of certain roots and weeds, they did not make a habit of drinking. Only once or twice a year did they go on a prolonged spree, beginning with hilarity and ending in stupefaction.

Now if they had been creatures of normal brain power, living in civilized communities, the reason of these periodic outbreaks could be attributed to boredom. But what do savages who have no mental processes above the animal plane know of boredom? Creatures without contrasts, without knowledge of any life beyond their own bit of earth, without imagination, without ambition, save, perhaps, to be the strong man of the tribe?

And yet it would seem that the desire for 'escape'

is born in them, that just so often they must burst the
invisible bonds that confine them and soar into a
realm where they can feel like the gods of whom they
have never heard. Moralists assert that all human
weaknesses are implanted merely that they may be
overcome by mind and character. But these savages
have but the rudiments of either. Like civilized man
they are more faulty in this respect than beasts that
walk on four legs, who certainly have no craving for
strong drink, nor excess of any kind.

The fact of the matter is that despite all that should
make for human happiness, especially in the antipo-
dean seas: climate, abundance of food, health, little
work, they all share with mankind that immutable
decree that no human being shall have anything but
tantalizing glimpses of happiness nor even content.

One may live to be a hundred yet cannot be said to
have reached maturity unless he has learned the
supreme lesson of life: that the inhabitants of Planet
Earth were endowed with an inferior brand of human
nature. Many rise to supernal heights of intellect or
genius, but in their depths all are a mess of virtues
and vices, aspirations and grovelling instincts, etcetera, etcetera.

Washington stands out in history as a monument to
character; this moral force within him was so powerful, it radiated such an import of spiritual authority
combined with an almost frozen aloofness, that the
temperature of the gayest room fell when he entered
it. And yet to those that knew him well he was as
frequently off his pedestal as on it.

Wagner, probably the greatest 'all-round' genius that ever lived, whose music inspires his listeners with the noblest sentiments (however transitory), and aspirations that beat against the confines of mortal life, was contemptible as a man. It is doubtful if he had a redeeming trait. And so on, ad infinitum. The list would fill a book.

And as if this unholy mess were not enough, Nature — to whom the Almighty, in our humble finite opinion, allowed far too much latitude — has endowed millions of her victims with the gift of imagination which enables them to conceive the goal of perfection and to strive for its attainment. To dream of complete and sustained happiness, especially between man and woman. To chase the will-o'-the-wisp of ideologies, only to see them materialize into dictatorships, tyrannies, enslavement, fanaticism. (As an illustration one has only to contrast communism with the communists!)

Still, it is permitted to wonder just what was in Nature's mind when Earth cooled and she worked out her recipe for its inhabitants in her laboratory. Perhaps she had peopled too many other planets with perfect beings; perfect in body, perfect in mind, in character, in spirit — all pretty much of a pattern, and slightly monotonous. But undoubtedly first-rate. No human weaknesses. The most perfect mortals that even her unbounded imagination could conceive.

Well, being slightly bored, and excited with the idea of concocting something different, of experimenting with mortal particles for the first time, perhaps, she turned out a new specimen whose psychological part was typified by its body; which is a perfect piece of mechanism as far down as the knees and a wobbly failure from there on. Ask any athlete.

I once went to a Hawaiian party in New York which was flagging a little despite the quaint and appetizing dishes, the leis of roses about our necks, the table that looked like a tropical jungle, and the native songs. One of the men stole out of the studio and returned later with a large bowl of what he called punch. I took one swallow and it felt like a living flame. I was up all night, quite convinced that my interior was being reduced to ashes, and my discomfort somewhat aggravated by the shrieks of a woman — of a distinguished historical family and prominent in Washington Society — having delirium tremens in the hall of my hotel. She was a large powerful woman and several men were attempting to drag her back to her suite. What a night!

The next afternoon my hostess called me up and asked if I had been affected by the punch. My reply was emphatic. She told me that her telephone had rung all morning, her erstwhile guests wanting to know if they had been poisoned and were ruined for life. She then rang up 'that devil, Joe Redding,' and discovered, between chuckles at the other end of the wire, that he had combined the contents of the wine closet in that bowl: red wine, white wine, champagne, beer, whiskey, brandy, gin, six different liqueurs, and, for good measure, half a bottle of alcohol he had found in the kitchen.

Well, when I remember that punch I seem to see Dame Nature, an expression of malicious glee on her face, stirring a viscid mess in one of her enormous vats. In it she had poured all the ingredients which distinguished her perfect beings on a million planets; and into each particle, so rounded, so beautiful in all its proportions, she had injected its exact opposite, to say nothing of minor but equally disintegrating forces. Injustice, intolerance, arrogance, selfishness, meanness, pettiness, weakness, hatred, jealousy, envy, intemperance, dishonesty, greed, cruelty, suspicion, carnality, self-pity, belittlement, sloth, stupidity, cowardice mental and physical, lust, covetousness, avarice, a love of power that transcends all other passions, bitterness, cynicism, disingenuousness, fear, egoism, a love of wickedness for its own sake, callousness, fanaticism — which is idealism gone haywire; and then, as a final curse, imagination.

Intolerance, jealousy, and greed would breed war between nations, and the merciless dominance of the strong over the weak in all walks of life. The spirit of injustice would pervade Planet Earth, an emanation that would make the word synonymous with Life itself, and persuade man of his helplessness in the toils of fate. Imagination, reflected the Lady of the Vats, combined with those fine, pure, noble, stable, exalted qualities of which she had by no means been niggardly, would give man glimpses of perfection toward which he would strive but never reach. Power would turn to ashes, love to indifference, hatred, owing to the corrosive power of suspicion and jealousy; or settle into a humdrum affection which was a poor substitute for the high plane of aspiration. Disillusionment would be the fate of all men, unless maniacal fanatics, and as imagination, owing to human limitations, would ever outrun man's hopes, desires, aspirations, so, save in unthinking youth, was he doomed to unhappiness during his mortal sojourn.

The unbecoming expression — on one so august — left the Dame's face as she labelled her brew Human Nature, and was succeeded by one of pity. But she had gone too far to relent, even were the wish there, which it wasn't; she tipped the vat over the edge of her star and poured its fateful contents down upon the waiting planet. 'Anyhow,' she reflected, 'they'll have some high old times.'

One wonders what Nature did for the next planet, cooled and waiting, sailing under her star. Appalled, perhaps, by what she had done to us, but no less interested, she may have brewed another mixture in which the good tipped the scales over the bad, eliminated injustice, permitted imagination to become a blessing instead of a curse, those who strove hard enough, to achieve perfection, and finished off with an enormous dose of common sense. In short, a superior brand of Human Nature, which would make ours look more cockeyed than ever.

Of course all this takes no account of religion, which to those born with faith, has been the supreme consolation of unfortunate Earthians. Not being religious myself, I can write on this subject with complete detachment. To those who devote their lives to the religious ideal it brings something more than consolation. I have known nuns who seemed to me to be completely happy. Remarkable women who combine intellect with mysticism, who may have heavy trials like other mortals, but are serene in their complete faith in the bliss that awaits them hereafter — and in the good they are doing on Earth. They must cause not only puzzlement but deep annoyance to the Old Lady of the Star.

I sometimes listen to the Catholic Hour on the radio, not only for the music, but because the priests often deliver interesting lectures rather than sermons. Recently a monsignor told his listeners that if happiness were to be found on earth man would not seek God. That pleasure is reserved for the next world. That here we have a greater capacity for pain than for pleasure. Very consoling, and long may religion flourish. No wonder the communists seek to exterminate religion, for it gives a spiritual independence to those who have faith that is a constant menace to the tyrants who would possess the souls as well as the bodies of their subjects.

But — to strike a lighter note — there is a good deal of fun to be got out of the Battle with Life, which begins with birth and ends only with death. Many go under, but millions do not. They fight to the end, and if they never quite get the best of Life at least Life does not get the best of them. To laugh at her, defy her, develop one's courage to the outermost limits, and pass out still defiant and unconquered —

that alone would make the Earthian sojourn worth while.

Not that there aren't a lot of other things to be got out of life besides fighting. Quite a lot.

CHAPTER V

DEFEATING

OLD AGE

SEVERAL handy little volumes could be written on the contrastive attitudes of human beings to 'Life' after the illusions of youths have ambled over the horizon, or been ground to dust in the mortar of reality.

In other words, when one no longer 'dreams' but *plans*, and, presupposing intelligence and courage, goes straight after what one most desires without ignoring the possibility of failure.

The seeds of failure may be innate, or they may reside in circumstances over which the most valiant and resourceful have no control; disease, war, earthquake, flood, financial débâcles, are but a few of the enemies which the clear-sighted planner must admit as possibilities to dodge or accept.

But it is they and their stock that have made history and are responsible for Progress (such as it is). They have taken a firm determined part in the battle of life, and usually survive, however battered.

Even those of less aggressive calibre, those who,

gifted in one of the arts, have little to do with forcing the pace of life or changing the current of history, must have courage, courage, and more courage to survive the inevitable disappointments, calculated assaults of the envious, and neuronic strain. But barring one of the unconquerable diseases, or accident, they do survive, and, like the others, evolve a philosophy, an attitude, that are wholly the outthrusts of personality and have little to do with Circumstance.

It is this attitude, beginning definitely in middle life — for it is liable to permutations before that — which is the most interesting single expression of human personality.

Before going further it is well to cast a backward glance at the outlook of the middle-aged, the elderly, the old, thirty or forty years ago, when there was a universal acceptance of the Biblical decree that man's normal life-span was three score and ten, and, above all, that the last third or quarter of this period was given over to a slow disintegration of the organs. The psychological effect of this belief was lamentable.

Today laboratory research has lengthened that span indefinitely. What with an almost universal knowledge of the laws of hygiene, avoidance of excess, balanced diet, close attention to the glandular constitution, sufficient sleep, and a yearly physical examination — with all this clinical information at the disposal of the race it is almost impossible for anyone to be 'run down' unless unbearably harassed economically, victims of unavoidable heart strain (I believe there are ninety-two heart ailments, so it must be difficult to avoid acquiring one of them), or vicious addictions.

Then we have the psychologists who, among other things, warn us against 'getting into a rut.' It was about twenty years ago that a woman of fifty told me the way to keep well after middle age had set in was never to change one's habits again. Today she is a miserable invalid mentally and physically, while older women who keep abreast of science are younger than she was at fifty. The rutters might just as well take an overdose of chloral hydrate and have done with it. The final result of too much routine is death in life.

The intelligent men and women alive today have a far better chance of — well, happiness is perhaps too big a word — but of fruition and adjustment than those of former generations. A healthy body at any age gives buoyancy, hope, the desire and the ability to accomplish, a continued interest in life both personal and general. It is for these reasons that the attitude toward life during advancing years must be vastly different from what it was a generation ago. Only the beaten — those that lack courage and determination — sink into their empty selves and watch the collapse of the mind into the ruin of the body.

What should make anyone think is the productiveness of certain men long past their prime. They may have known nothing of the laws of health, but they were either naturally abstemious and balanced, or, according to endocrinologists, they automatically renewed their youth-preserving hormones, secreted by the ductless glands, and which may be artificially stimulated today. To quote but a few instances: Sophocles was enchanting the Athenians with new plays in his late eighties. Verdi did his best work between fifty-eight and eighty. Goethe was still a flowering genius at the age of eighty-five.

Fashion has done much for women psychologically. It is no longer the inexorable custom for a woman to 'dress her age,' and while any woman of mature years is a fool, and more than looks her age, if she dresses like a flapper, if she is always perfectly dressed in the fashion of the moment she has nothing to fear from younger rivals. A new hat is a cocktail, and adroitly applied make-up renews her self-confidence every morning.

Some time ago that brilliant artist Nell Brinkley presented us with a very striking but rather misleading picture. On the right were four pretty little morons, engaged in an elaborate process of make-up, and proudly exhibiting their legs. On the left were five historic ladies: Rosa Bonheur, Madame de Staël, Madame de Sévigné, Madame Roland, Sarah Bernhardt. All famous for mental activity of one sort or another that gave them a place in history, and each wearing an expression of lofty superiority.

Of course the poor little dolls on the right were an awful example of what may happen to a girl if she thinks of nothing but lipstick, rouge, nail polish, mascara, and legs, although I doubt if an inspired surgical genius could inject any brains into those particular heads. They look as if they had been emptied by a vacuum cleaner in Nature's own laboratory.

But the other intimation is all wrong, if, as I take it, Miss Brinkley's argument is that those historic ladies regarded make-up with intellectual disdain; save only Sarah, who, being an actress, was driven to grease paint.

I do not believe it. Bonheur, perhaps, being a masculine type, may have been content to put all her paint on canvas; but the others were one-hundred-per-cent female; and, with rare exceptions, women of brains are as full of natural vanity and are possessed by as natural a desire to command the admiration of men as any poor little moron whose only asset is youth.

There are old fogies and young fogies, but, taking them by and large, men have always been susceptible to enhanced charms. Perhaps they thrill to that subtle appeal to masculine approval; perhaps make-up deepens the mystery of woman; or gives her something of the lure of women of the stage; or perhaps it is merely a faint echo from the deep pits of the subconscious memory of those centuries B.C. when men made up and women did not.

There is an alluring softness in artistic make-up, and the intelligent women of today take as much pains with their appearance as the baby dolls. Or should. If they don't they look their age and lose just that much of their power, even over their sons, and society in general. One sees in fashionable clubs old relics of the Victorian Age, who pride themselves upon never having even powdered their noses, disdain the changing fashions for their shapeless bodies, stoop more from laziness than age, and wear flat-heeled buttoned boots. They feel superior and look like hell.

Between the Steinach reactivation treatment, beauty parlors, cosmetic surgeons, patronized chiefly by grateful actresses, and the many admirable creams and make-up materials to be found in any first-class drugstore, no woman has any excuse not to look (and feel) twenty or even thirty years younger than her actual years.

And what would not Madame de Staël, the most overpoweringly intellectual woman of her age, have given for a beauty parlor? She was extremely plain but full of feminine vanity and impulses, and, when forty-five, married a man twenty-three years younger than herself. Well, a woman of any time or mental calibre is a fool to do that, but be sure that when she does she will keep the man longer with make-up than without it.

Ninon de l'Enclos had men sighing for her favors when she was past seventy, but if she hadn't invented that famous beauty mask of hers the men would have sighed elsewhere. Even when women have reached the age when they are glad to be relieved of the predatory male they suffer no loss of vanity; that is, if they have intelligence enough to know the value of 'looks.' Of course the older they grow the cleverer they must be about artifice, but I have never yet seen a woman past thirty-five who was not improved by it.

But there is one lamentable experience all must

experience, and accept as best they can: the death of friends — who were too indolent, or too unprogressive, to avail themselves of the beneficences of modern science; or were the victims of some *Titanic* disaster, or crash into a mountain-side. Barring poverty this is the direst calamity the survivors must endure. The loss of every friend is a tragedy and one no mortal may escape.

Edith Wharton, in her autobiography, found life infinitely sad from this viewpoint alone, and her compensations in books, work, and the little daily pleasures. No doubt she expressed the attitude of many less distinguished.

Also, no doubt, there are many like myself, in whom the loss of friends arouses some obscure fighting instinct, and even a personal resentment against the dead. They ignored the first symptoms of high blood pressure, to say nothing of the hundred and one other enemies prowling about the blood stream and nibbling at the organs, and were skidded out of life ten, twenty years before their time.

Well, there is nothing to do about it save tighten your belt, make new friends, make Life yield as many interests as possible. Thrice blessed are those that have a daily and congenial task, more particularly in one of the arts. And clubwomen, with their organizations either cultural or political, have an almost cruel advantage over middle-aged and elderly widows whose children are married, whose income is too limited to permit travelling and social diversions, and who exist, not live, in the gray fog of monotony and trivial routine. Well, even they may wake up in time and form clubs of their own, find some more satisfying 'escape' than a detective story a day from the circulating library. Anyone with spirit fights his enemies instead of lying down and shuddering under the soles of their feet. And Life is the most persistent and pitiless of man's enemies. To fight and confound her is the antidote for all ills.

CHAPTER VI

WORK FETISH

TOO much of a fetish is made, in the United States of America, of 'work for work's sake.' Rich men, after giving their sons the expensive education that develops (or should develop) a taste for the finer things of life, force them into the parental firm, or bid them 'go out and make good on their own,' as befits the American tradition. Very often even the sons of plutocrats are so imbued with this traditional belief that they will voluntarily enter the family business at the foot of the ladder and concentrate upon reaching the top, consigning their intellectual accretions to oblivion. (I leave the dissipated out of account, as they would be worthless in any case.)

What is the result? These prospective inheritors of wealth (great or moderate) spend the best years of their youth chasing the superfluous dollar, animated by the sordid conviction that money is the most important thing in life; and growing progressively duller in all else.

No country can reach a high stage of civilization without a leisure class, and the larger the country the larger it should be. The United States should have at least two million men, aside from college circles, authors and scientists, who avowedly devote their lives to the steady development of the intellect, the esthetic sense, general culture, the art of conversation; varied, of course, by the lighter amusements and pleasures.

With a young leisure class, then a mature leisure class, interested in everything that gives meaning to the word 'civilization,' we might even, if a certain number of them entered public life, develop a class of real statesmen, to offset the hordes of greedy and selfish politicians who are the curse of this country. The statesmen in Washington today may be counted on the fingers of one hand, and I am thankful to say that a Californian, Hiram Johnson, is one of them.

It would also solve the problem for those women of cultivated minds who now are forced to find mental companionship in the society of other women. Today men come home at night either tired out or with their heads still full of business, 'cases,' or what not, and with no desire whatever to turn to the cultural side of life. They bore their wives and their wives bore them. I am finding fault only with the wealthy, of course, who could afford to slow down or retire. Too many men have to give all their energies to support their families in comfort, educate their children, and keep up a good front. Little can be expected of them; but even these unfortunates, gazing from afar on a large leisure class giving meaning and beauty to life, might make some slight effort at emulation.

Nor will this great machine, the United States, slow down. There will, for a generation or two at least, be thousands of young men forced to work as hard as machines and upset economic conditions will permit. But they too, under a more enlightened statesmanship, may look forward to retiring when they have a reasonable sum invested, instead of drying up their hormones in pursuit of the elusive 'million.'

Unemployment at the top is one of the crying needs of this country.

CHAPTER VII

SENSE OF HUMOR

THIS is not a purely personal outbreak, for I feel sure that all women who are a step above the average feel as I do. Those who object to too many 'I's' may substitute 'We's.'

Will some psychologist tell me why it is that although I have a sense of humor that has preserved my mental balance throughout a long and unpeaceful career, and a keen appreciation of comedy, I am bored to tears (I mean this literally, with no desire to revive obsolete slang) by so-called humorists in print, on the stage, screen, and radio?

There are certain men 'on the air' who, I am told, command enormous salaries for their popular brand of humorous entertainment. It not only bores me excruciatingly to listen to them, but inspires me with a sympathetic feeling of fatigue. I can almost hear their mental panting.

And these men have brains, no doubt of that. If they choose to employ them entertaining the brainless and raking in a fortune a year that is nobody's business but their own. The appalling thing is that millions of voters all over the land are shrieking with asinine laughter whenever these men are on the air.

Brainless? Well, not always. I used to hear one of the cleverest men I knew, a man of power in the financial and political world, as well as a lover of good literature, laugh uproariously at the silliest captions (this was in the silent days), to say nothing of slapstick; and I have no doubt that men of the same mental calibre listen with twitching ears and quivering mirth to this new type of entertainer.

In New York several years ago I attended the first night of a thing called *Hot-Cha*, where at least two thirds of the men in the audience were eminent in one way or another. The performance was a dreary rehash of old vaudeville stuff, antique wise-cracks, all held together by a foolish and tenuous plot, but the men howled with delight and applauded like small boys at their first circus. The women, I noticed, were less amused.

Women generally are less responsive to this sort of thing, and while I am not for a moment arguing (despite the many exceptions) that women on the whole are more intelligent than men, certain it is that they are fundamentally more serious, men more childish.

If this 'reaction' on my part to popular humor were recent it would not be worth mentioning. I should assume that life and a highly varied experience had made me more fastidious, or blunted my sense of the ridiculous. But real humor appeals to me as spontaneously as ever; I find myself laughing out loud at comedy either on the stage or between the covers of a book. And here, I may add, I hold it a mark of shallow criticism to call any writer 'great' (unless his themes are as tragic as those of the fifth century B.C.

tragic poets) who is devoid of a sense of humor.

No, there is nothing new in my acute boredom when at the mercy of the professional humorist. When I was quite young, and indeed, for long after, we used to have many 'farces,' plays that were laboriously funny from beginning to end and kept their audiences shrieking with laughter. As I saw and heard those poor puppets working like navvies, begging for a laugh, I progressed from mere boredom into a state of depression. I seemed to be stifling in the folds of a black wet cloud. The next stage was melancholy, growing more and more acute. Finally I would make an excuse to leave the theatre, lest I disgrace myself by bursting into tears.

Humor should be incidental, not continuous. Like salt, spices, and sweets, a superfluity revolts the palate. We have a few commentators on the radio who can be suddenly and delightfully humorous, and I notice that these exceptions are long-lived, so we must have a large intelligent public as well as a moronic; so why complain? One need not listen to them, any more than one is obliged to read trash.

Perhaps in time women will train their plastic young sons to appreciate the difference between humor and a mere sense of the ridiculous. I think it was Aristotle who said that a sense of the ridiculous was a sign of superficiality as the ridiculous was always on the surface. How long would any of these 'funny' entertainers last if they discarded burlesque and delved into the more subtle depths of humor? Not an hour — with their present admirers.

CHAPTER VIII

GOLD-DIGGERS

THE day may come when we will all be regimented (ugly but coercive word), and I have been wondering to what use the talents of a certain subdivision of the She Sex will be forcibly applied. Those of us who have a gift for one of the arts will no doubt be graciously permitted to work in the interest and to the glorification of the new ocracy; and, although there might be rebellion and heartburning for a time, such is the adaptability of the human race that we might, even deprived of independence, find some measure of happiness in the exercise of a gift from the gods. And who knows to what superhuman proportions intellectual subtlety might be developed? *There* would be a game that might make life worth living again.

But what I am concerned about is the gold-diggers. They too have a peculiar talent, and derive from a long ancestral line. What is more, they have held their own all through recorded history with its innumerable changes and vicissitudes.

The most notable were the hetaerae of ancient Athens, particularly in the fifth century B.C. As the respectable girls were given no mental education whatever, being merely trained in housewifely duties, and men were driven to find companionship in one another, quite a number of clever and enterprising ladies born in a humbler sphere cultivated their minds as well as their persons in order to be tolerated by men who scorned the society of pretty fools of their own class but were easily persuaded to gratify the expensive whims of women who could talk politics, art, a little philosophy, and were at the same time feminine enough to pluck their eyebrows, touch up their hair, curb unseemly expansion, and make the most of what little variety in dress there was. (Aspasia, by the way, was *not* a hetaera, and as I am tired of the reiterations of the ignorant, when writing of that class, I take this opportunity once more to state what is well known to scholars: that she was a wealthy girl of Miletus who, after the death of her father, came to Athens with the architect Hippodamus, invited by Pericles to rebuild the Piraeus. Not having been born in Attica she was a 'foreigner' and therefore could not marry Pericles, who had divorced his wife, but, alas, could not abrogate a law he had sponsored himself. She became what today would be called a morganatic wife, but the profoundest delvers into that period have been unable to discover that she had lovers. Her independent fortune alone would have protected her. And aside from her devotion to Pericles she seems to have been all intellect.)

The hetaerae of Corinth were more closely allied to what is euphemistically called The Oldest Profession in the World, but those exceptional women of

Athens had their similitudes in more recent eras,
particularly in France, where certain still famous
women fitted themselves uniquely into the lives of
princes and other eminent patrons and were amply
rewarded. There was a magnificence about those
great courtesans which must have been exceptional,
for surely there were many more of whom history
has no record, but who, we doubt not, looked down
with lofty contempt upon the professional harlot.

Time went on. Opportunities multiplied. Riches
piled up. Pretty young things who chose the easiest
way found less and less spur to cultivate their cunning
little brains into pseudo-intellects, and hence have
been classified more simply as gold-diggers.

Excluding girls of good family who 'marry for
money,' they may be divided into three tribes: those
who manoeuvre men into a position which enables
them to sue for breach of promise; those who go in
deliberately for the alimony racket; the larger and
more innocuous class who fasten upon rich old fools
or rich young fools and get all they can out of them
while the getting is good.

So fanatical is that wing of reformers who have
specialized upon the Alimony Racket, they have
persuaded themselves that every girl, no matter how
well bred, who divorces a rich husband after only
a few years of matrimony married him with the
deliberate intention of suing for alimony and independence. But that is preposterous. The majority of
girls fall sincerely in love, and if they fall out again
later they naturally want to begin life over again via

the divorce court. Many of them do not ask for alimony unless they have children, and not then if they have an independent income. But many more have no recourse but to return to the paternal roof, and I do not believe it is even guessed how often it is the father who brings down his heavy hand and forces the discarded husband to share his burden.

But there is no doubt that certain hard-boiled young women, lacking the advantages of breeding and social position, cast their spell over unwary young men susceptible to the matrimonial lure, with an eye to nothing but future independence. I read the other day of one young woman who was enjoying alimonic support from no less than three ex-husbands.

Still cleverer are the breed who jockey even sophisticated men into writing them compromising letters, which are the usual base of a breach of promise suit. Cleverer, but as this subdivision is vulgar to the core they must have the gift of allure in excess to delude any man of normal judgment.

Therefore several states have taken steps to protect men, poor helpless infants, and doubtless many more will write a law against breach of promise on their statute books. It is quite possible that this law will be followed by one forbidding alimony in all but exceptional cases, for too many men are afraid to marry, not knowing on what trivial ground they may be divorced and compelled to pay alimony. Quite recently a judge granted a woman a divorce from her husband because he nagged her, asserting that 'nagging was a woman's prerogative'!

All very well, but what will these gold-diggers do if some dire ism prevails? I don't see them trundling baby carriages or cooking in community kitchens. Their only use to the regimenters will be to spread propaganda among the unreconciled, betray others, make a public fool of some man in power, or form a chorus in the background singing 'Be good and you'll be happy.' And all without a cent of profit.

How long would they last? Quite possibly the only survivors would be those with exceptional minds, who would revive the traditions of the ancient hetaerae. Times Circle!

CHAPTER IX
WHY PEOPLE LOVE
DICTATORS AND
KINGS

I HAVE descended to blackmail but once in my life. I was in Paris in 1916 when the President of the Red Cross founded the *oeuvre* Le Bienêtre des Blessés, and appointed the Marquise d'Andigné (Madeleine Goddard of Rhode Island) its president. I afterward became the American president, as I have related in 'Adventures of a Novelist,' but at that time all that was asked of me was to rouse public interest in the United States; then money would come pouring in — it was fondly hoped — to buy delicacies for the wounded, who, it would seem, preferred to die rather than survive on the milk and eggs of the *petit régime*. I had been increasingly desirous of visiting the War Zone, but had been assured by all to whom I had spoken, both French and American, that it was quite impossible.

Here was my chance. I told Madame d'Andigné

and the Committee — very firmly — that if they wanted me to write both intelligently and harrowingly of the wounded I must take a trip through the War Zone where most of the hospitals were situated. The American public demanded first-hand news or nothing. Wires were immediately pulled.

This involved some six or eight visits to the Ministry of War, for it is impossible to hurry the French. The official to whom I was turned over was a silk merchant from Lyons, mobilized for the duration of the War. And, like all Frenchmen, he would talk if guns were thundering at the walls. Whenever I left his office I found a crowded anteroom full of scowling men ready to annihilate me. My official knew quite well they were there, but he had found a new and interested listener for his hobby and mere business could wait.

Although a prosperous merchant and a good bourgeois, he was an ardent monarchist. Before the War he had belonged to a royalist league with members all over France, who hoped to restore the Bourbons, met periodically, and made peaceful demonstrations — generally, I believe, under a statue of Jeanne d'Arc. Now, however, the Great Cause was in abeyance, for La Patrie came before all and political divergencies were in storage — for the time being.

After he had assured me, as briefly as he knew how, that my petition was progressing favorably with the mysterious powers in the background, he would switch to his favorite subject and talk for perhaps half an hour. Although he used many words and embellished his theme with historical parallels and lofty aspirations, the simple and sacred principles upon which monarchism was founded may be put into one brief paragraph.

To wit. God is the ruler of the Universe. The father is the ruler of the family (when he is, thought I). Therefore is it not both natural and wise that the state should be ruled by a king?

French logic is justly famous.

I grew restive at times, but he expressed himself with such precision, such point, he was manifestly so sincere and high-minded, this merchant from Lyons, that I had little desire to interrupt him, and, indeed, he gave me much food for thought.

Of course, as far as natural instinct is concerned there was a good deal to be said for his argument — instinct being merely inherited memory. As soon as men ceased to live in caves and formed any sort of community, the strongest among them assumed the leadership either in forthright or devious ways. As civilization progressed and what is now known as Europe and Asia split up into different states, each had its ruler, its revolutions, its wars. If Democracy reared its aspiring head and prevailed now and again, the ablest and most ambitious character soon rose to the top, or a stronger marched in from outside.

Certainly one of the lessons of history is that the majority of human beings want to be governed. They do not want to think, certainly not for others. Were man universally a thinking animal, discontent, instead of making for Progress, would have reduced the world to chaos long since. Nature knew what she was about when she limited the number of individual thinkers, reformers, doers. Above all, doers. Fortunately all the masses ask is to live in peace; to love, marry, raise families, make a good living, accumulate something for their heirs if possible; and bless the form of government that permits these beneficences.

And yet the idealists go on prating of human 'equality'; something that never has been, is not, and never will be.

Not the least of the several causes that led to the French Revolution was the unrest of the oppressed peasantry and small wage-earners that had been smouldering for a hundred years or more. There was, seemingly, no one in Russia to read the warning of the French Revolution, not even the bourgeoisie whose prototypes had played such an important part in that famous upheaval. No one with the gift to look backward as well as forward. No one in monarchical Spain. We in the United States have been more fortunate — for the present, at least.

The German Revolution that sent the Kaiser to Doorn and gave the new Republic its opportunity to taste the sweets of democracy was not caused by an oppressed bourgeoisie or proletariat, and might never have occurred but for the World War. I lived in Munich for six years — until 1909 — and travelled about the country a good deal. Franklin C. Palm, in that valuable work, 'The Middle Classes Then and Now,' relates that the little business man (*petit bourgeois*) was restive because he expected to be crushed between Big Business above and the wage-earners below, but there was no evidence of it during my time in the *atmosphere* of Germany. Taking them by and large no more contented people ever lived. All the thinking was done at the top; within reasonable limits they could do as they pleased (*lèse majesté* was easy to avoid); there were all but free hospitals and clinics for the working classes, cheap seats at the opera and theatres, countless restaurants and beer halls to accommodate all purses.

In a great crowded city like Berlin there was bound to be a certain amount of poverty, but there was little elsewhere. In Munich, a city of five hundred thousand inhabitants, there was not a slum, no one ever saw a beggar on the streets, there was practically no crime. On the frequent holidays the broad Ludwigstrasse swarmed with young men and women from outlying villages, in gala attire, enjoying themselves in their rather slow and heavy way. Of course there were socialist groups, but their power was negligible at that time. There have been few countries so cleverly governed as the German Empire.

But even Germany, at the apex of the world intellectually, and expert in inventing soothing-syrups, had its quota of fools at the top. And what for millions was as ideal an existence as can be wrought in this rickety world, has gone for a century, perhaps for ever.

And what have they in its place? After the long struggle of the Republic against overwhelming economic conditions, followed by a period of grinding poverty and utter despair, the people have, if not welcomed with guttural enthusiasm, at least accepted a totalitarian government, that if unable to restore the old modest affluence, will once more, they hope, give them the blessed sense of unity they enjoyed under the Kaisers. Emperor or Dictator, it is all one to them. The thinking is done at the top. Heil Hitler!

The Germans, like all peoples that have passed through a long agonizing experience, sigh and gratefully lean on the strong man, just as the devout during some personal disaster pray with increased fervor, a man who falls ill sends for his doctor, children run for the shelter of the paternal roof when menaced by big bad boys or vicious dogs.

So, my friend of the War Office was logical enough. Republics, democracies, have been erected out of monarchical ruins again and again, or rebelled, as we did, from a stupid parent; succeeded brilliantly — or otherwise — for a time; then, if disintegrated by war or internal factions which the authorities have not had the wit to uproot while there was yet time, have swung back along the curve and almost begged for that centralized power which, in these days, drives a weary people straight into the cast-iron arms of a Dictator.

We Americans are passionately attached to the ideology of States Rights and to the Constitution in general. Unless certain internal forces disrupt them — to which poverty is but distantly related — the Constitution is safe, and we shall remain a people free in thought and action, untrammelled by too many laws. But if those forces, ninety-nine per cent of whom are, little as they know it (so cleverly propagandized are they), down on their silly knees praying for fascism or communism, totalitarianism and a dictator, are not curbed in time — then good-bye to Democracy.

Far back in history men talked of a 'benevolent despotism' as the ideal form of government. Yes, when you can get it. Even Mussolini, the most acceptable of the dictators, and a man of enormous brain power, who has in an incredibly short time restored Italy to her old place among the powers, and hypnotized the greater number of its people, could hardly be called benevolent. Hitler has pulled Germany out of the slough of despond and is abnormally clever — but benevolent, ha! ha! The less said of Stalin the better. Whether France will have a permanent dictator or not remains to be seen. Of all countries she needs one the most.

The unpalatable truth, as regards ourselves, is, as Hamilton, the greatest genius in American history well knew, that the majority of human beings are merely animals walking on their hind legs; and therein lies the success of leaders with a messianic complex, or mere racketeers. Any man with a gift for leadership, a devouring ambition, a ruthless will, a compelling personality, can count on the sheep and is a potential danger to the American Constitution. The hope lies in a Congress that will douse him with cold water just so often, remind him that he is a Servant of the People, and keep him firmly in his place.

Even second-class brains are none too abundant, and as for 'soul,' with which sentimentalists would endow anything that walked on two legs instead of four, it is one of the rare gifts, as rare as genius for any of the major arts. The ideal despot should combine soul, the highest order of intellect, which includes imagination, a strong but flexible will, a profound understanding of human nature, the courage to know when to be afraid, and the irresistible magnet of leadership. Then, if still able to wear his original hatband, he will lead a harassed and bewildered people out from the jungles of despair into a land flowing with the fulfilment of every reasonable wish. The job will be to keep them where he wants them. But we'll be civilized in five thousand years or so.

Will the French ever fulfil the hopes of my good bourgeois and have another king?

In the spring of 1925 I was in Paris and lunched one Sunday at the d'Andigné's. There was a young woman of the Old Régime present who was quite the most violent monarchist I have ever met. She lifted her voice and waved her arms as she assured me the Revolution would occur not later than July of that year. I think she gave me the date and the hour. After lunch I asked the Marquis if she knew what she was talking about. He was a wise old gentleman and shrugged. 'There is always talk of a revolution in France,' he said. 'But if there is one thing we do *not* want it is another Bourbon.'

On the following Sunday afternoon my daughter

and I took a taxi to Père-Lachaise, as she had never seen that famous cemetery. When we arrived we found a milling crowd in the little square before the gates, and saw another surging up the broad road between the tombs within. Every man wore what looked like a red clover leaf in his buttonhole. There were two gendarmes present to keep the peace, but no crowd could have been more orderly.

'Who are all these people?' I asked the driver. 'Why that red emblem, and why the gendarmes?'

He leaned backward and putting his hand before his mouth replied in a hoarse whisper:

'It's the Revolution!'

CHAPTER X
A COURSE IN LIFE
AND HUMAN NATURE

PROBABLY the most picturesque suicide of modern times was that of two girls who, having lost their lovers in an aviation disaster, rented an airplane, soared up into the blue, leaped out, and catapulted to earth. They were doubtless anything but picturesque sights when picked up, but it was a fine romantic gesture, and all the world talked about them for a day.

That was several years ago, and it is interesting to wonder what their attitude to life would be now if they had borne their grief as many another has done. All impressions fade with time, and never as rapidly as in this crowded roaring multifarious century. Doubtless both those young women would be the mother of at least one sturdy brat in a lot pleasantly commonplace or diversified by clubs, politics, social duties, or art, their former sweethearts a sentimental memory, if that. For the irony of life is not that you cannot forget but that you can.

In times past Americans used to hear a good deal of New England spinsters who 'cherished a memory until death,' but now we have reason to believe that was because they lived in small communities whence most of the young men had fled, and they never had a second chance. Nevertheless, there are different ways of being happy, and they may have found an enduring spiritual satisfaction in living on one idealized memory, unknown to the comfortable mothers of families.

I fancy that breed of old maids is extinct. Today women even in villages have multiple interests and little time to think about empty hearts, even when spinsters. With political and business clubs, clubs for discussing the new and important books, jobs, quick transit, moving picture houses, the radio, their time is as well filled as that of the once-envied male. They have outgrown illusions, and unless neurasthenics and unadaptable to any conditions, are fairly well contented with life, or just sufficiently critical to be firm in their determination to improve it.

But those are the mature. The danger spot is girls, for the young look upon happiness as their right, cherish illusions, live too intensely in the moment to be capable of foresight, to have any but the most rudimentary knowledge of human nature; they are the ones who so often wreck their lives during some turmoil of the senses, or snuff out the life-spark altogether. True, many live to love another day, but others are warped forever.

It would be a good idea if every college — or even high school — had a course in what might be called Life and Human Nature. It would rank in importance with mathematics, which gives the mind elasticity and breadth; with history, which supplies a background for comparison; with philosophy, which contributes balance and poise.

Girls, in particular, should have it pounded into them that while life itself is transitory enough, human emotions are even more so. The French have a wise proverb: *Tout lasse, tout casse, tout passe* — all things wear out, all things break, all things pass. No profounder truth was ever compressed into six words, and, if it were part of every education, the edge of those inevitable tragedies to come would be conveniently blunted. Stepmother Nature should also be shown up in her true colors. If girls could be convinced that all She is after is the continuance of the race, that youthful passion in particular is merely a poison brewed by that old harridan in her laboratory to victimize the young and fruitful, they might do a little self-analysis, take a wicked delight in thwarting her. And perhaps not.

We have heard a good deal since the War about the contempt of the young for old-fashioned romance, that they are hard-boiled and cynical. It is true they have cultivated a hard shell, but it is adjustable. Underneath they are unchanged. They not only go on marrying for love, occasionally die for love as we have seen, but ninety per cent of the songs on the radio are warblings of love 'and love alone'; many an otherwise fine moving picture is mutilated by the demand for 'love interest,' whether it has any place there or not (as witness the picture founded on the life of Clive, as ruthless and desentimentalized a creature as history ever produced; to say nothing of that little Hollywood flapper in her cute modern clothes and marcelled hair that damnified 'Lost Horizon'); and the enormous sale of magazines whose stories are all pulsing emotion and no brains. To be sure this fodder is mainly consumed by unintelligent women of commonplace lives who yearn for vicarious thrills, but they also have their influence on youth and feed its inherited desire for romantic happiness. Such a course as I have recommended might neutralize to some extent an influence that fertilizes the plastic mind with the wrong sort of chemicals; and an equally beneficent work might be a reformation of screen, radio, and light fiction; for girls, too, become middle-aged with time, and while demanding a reasonable amount of love and sex would demand them as but two of the major interests that life has to offer. As for stickiness, it would be hissed out of court.

But, of course, in suicide there are other factors. Youth is naturally dramatic as well as romantic. Death in its most prosaic form has an element of drama, for does not that final curtain go down upon the eternal mystery? A thousand times enhanced then is spectacular death: death in the reckless heroism of the battlefield, death on a submarined *Lusitania*, death in a flaming torch on high. Even death to evade the torments of cancer, the self-directed bullet of so many unhappy men when the business world is crashing about them. Death in the spotlight, and the whole world quivers in response, and forgets.

In others suicide is as often more of a grand gesture, an abrupt extension of the ego, as the sudden impulse of a mind disordered by mental or physical suffering?

It is not to be inferred that those unfortunate girls who leaped from an airplane gave a thought to the front page, or even to making a spectacular exit. They chose that route because an unkind fate had forced it upon their lovers, and lethargic bodies sent poisoned blood into brains already unbalanced by brooding. But subconsciously drama did its work. A magnificent death had its compensations.

To have reasoned with those distracted girls would have been fruitless. There is no reasoning power left in a poisoned brain. But brains are not liable to miasma whose metaphysical part, the mind, is not neurotic in structure and has been trained from childhood in the sound principles of common sense; of elevating the facts of life above the transient emotions. But even a French cynic in his most logical mood could not have persuaded those two girls that ten years hence they might be the fond mothers of a brood, retaining in memory little more than the names of their youthful lovers.

And ... alas — how often do we observe some woman of middle age who has lost the husband to whom she has been devoted for thirty years or more, and whose death left her inconsolable for some months, possibly a year, suddenly blossom out and look twenty years younger. A new interest in dress. Discreet visits to the beauty salon, an almost imperceptible sliding from the past into the present with all its interests, barely noted before.

In all but the flabby it is a natural instinct to begin life over again when the opportunity offers. Even those dutiful — and truly affectionate — wives realize, when freedom comes, that the man has been an incubus, that he symbolized monotony, repression, lack of individual development. It had never occurred to them that they might have a future. No word in the dictionary has the beckoning glamour of that word Future. Unknown possibilities, new and multiple interests, adventure; above all, independence, freedom.

Even with no desire to marry again the very word Future causes a rejuvenation of the spirit, a mental jig, that would transform their appearance with no aid from the beauty parlor. It is enough to realize that one is never too old to begin life over again.

CHAPTER XI

OUR SCHOOLS

URING the Depression certain states placed their public schools on a half-day basis. In San Francisco, coincidentally, there was a sudden awakening to an always potential danger and architects were commissioned to overhaul flimsy old school buildings and make them earthquake-proof. The result in one respect, in both California and those other states, was worthy of a broadcast, but—as 'news'—was stillborn.

As to California. It would be odd indeed if the folding and faulting of the Miocene Age that still agitates our Coast should affect the public school system of that state some two million years later. And yet this may well be. There were already a number of public school buildings in San Francisco as solid as the modern structures that resisted the major upheaval of 1906, and as the education of the young must be as uninterrupted as possible the authorities conceived a system of doubling-up. Such commodious and thoroughly equipped buildings as the Galileo High School, among others, accommodating three thousand students, instead of spreading their daily dosage of learning from 8.30 until 3, with an hour for lunch, crowded all their classes between 8 and 12, and turned over the classrooms to the temporarily homeless young persons for four hours in the afternoon.

The result was satisfactory in more ways than one. The morning teachers and pupils had a hot lunch at home and an unbroken afternoon; the guests found equal profit. This half day of leisure for all went on for over a year, and the question arises: Why may not such a system be maintained?

Pupils, particularly of high schools, should have half a day of leisure. If the proletariat thirty-hour-a-week ideal is converted into reality more and more ambitious young men and women will want longer hours for reading and other forms of self-improvement, perhaps to begin at once on a business course.

Leisure in this class should develop possibilities hardly guessed before, and add to the sum of American intelligence and usefulness. Instead of coming home tired out at three or later, the students would be as fresh in the afternoon as their alternates in the morning.

Furthermore: it is not only the proletarian youth that attend the public schools; many other boys have been sent to them for years, because, as a rule, the standard is higher and the discipline more severe than in the private academies; and, during the depression, parents were forced to reorganize their budgets and sent their little girls to be educated at the expense of the city; and were enthusiastic over their progress in everything but accent!

If the depression had persisted they might have hesitated to send their daughters to 'the High' owing to the stories of misconduct among pupils that periodically agitate the public. What the authorities, when they wake up, will do about this somewhat important matter remains to be seen. One solution would be to put an end to co-education among the very young. Propinquity and opportunity have a good deal to do with morals at that age.

The teachers appear to be estimable, but really I do think that those guilty of the horrible Am-u-u-r-r-ican accent should be as disqualified to train the plastic mind as if they were deficient in grammar or 'those high moral principles.' Children of educated parents, who otherwise received admirable instruction in the public grammar schools, acquired the wide-open vowels and nasal twang that made the very spine of their elders shudder. Nothing could be done about it at the time, for children are imitative little monkeys with susceptible ears. The ears of the teachers had been blunted long since.

A pity. Those children were rescued in time, but what of the little proletarians who may, years hence, be called to the highest places in the land — to say nothing of possible careers on radio, stage, and screen? Well, we have all heard senators, representatives, governors, party managers, on the radio, who, we are brave enough to guess, were educated in the public schools; so, unless something is done about it, we know what to expect from the rising generation.

Bright children of all classes are enthusiastic about these public schools, and, aside from their vulgarized accents, have reason to be; there are none better in the world. Personally I have but one other criticism to make. I was questioning a young Chinese not long since and was surprised to learn that civics and history were not compulsory; that pupils made their own choice.

It seemed to me this showed a great lack of vision. Surely the young should not only be taught history but encouraged to read it at home. History is the background of life. With a fuller knowledge of it our politicians would make fewer mistakes, and the people realize that in many respects the past has been worse than the present, that bad times pass, that time readjusts all things, and the world continues to survive and flourish. They would discount the dismal prophets who warn us that the next war in Europe will end its civilization. What is the history of Europe but war? Let them recall the Hundred Years' War, the Thirty Years' War, the Seven Years' War, the Napoleonic Wars, to mention but a few that have shaken Europe to its foundations. It even survived the last, known as the Great War. History marches on.

As for civics: after the student has acquired some knowledge of those of past civilizations, it wouldn't be a bad idea to familiarize him with contemporary governments, city, state, and federal; and with contemporary personalities in every part of the world. For the latter what better source of information than the fascinating and authentic books written during the last few years by newspapermen. John Gunther's 'Inside Europe'; Vincent Sheehan's 'Personal History'; Wythe Williams's 'Dusk of Empire'; John Whittaker's 'And Fear Came' (a lamentable title that ruined the prospects of a delightful book); Webb Miller's 'I Found No Peace'; Miles Vaughn's 'Covering the Far East'; Linton Wells's 'Blood on the Moon'; Mowrer's 'Germany Puts the Clock Back'; Frazier Hunt's 'One American'; the valuable book Walter Duranty will give to the world when he has said his last farewell to Russia.

And — on a pedestal all by itself, that classic of Lillian Mowrer's, 'Journalist's Wife.'

India too is worth studying. Louis Bromfield is not a journalist, but a great novelist, and in his work 'The Rains Came' he has given the best novel ever written about India, and as informative as it is enchanting.

Sometime since I came upon an astonishing paragraph in my morning newspaper. A college president had given to the press the result of a 'quiz,' the answers by *students of political science*. Here it is!

An epicurean is one who believes in
the Epic Plan of Upton Sinclair.
Vandalism is being without work.
Colliery is a disease of hogs.
Biennium is silver money.
Tirade: three together.
Innuendo: one who sets fires.
Nippon: a river in France.
Domicile: very mild.
Shambles: wanders from the subject.
Criterion: place to buy hats.

This news item was entitled *Oh, Education!* Oh,

indeed! With no explanatory preamble one would have assumed these questions had been put to grammar-school pupils of tender age, and been faintly amused at the result. It would have occurred to no one to insult 'the highs,' much less students who are supposed to be pretty thoroughly grounded before they are graduated into a college of one of our universities. How, then, is it possible that young men with such a low order of mentality were able to pass the requisite examinations?

Surely there is something wrong here.

One must assume this college is not alone in having a certain percentage of inferior minds in its student body. There must be hundreds — to be conservative — of young men wasting the efforts and money of parents and state. I say nothing of the high school teachers who allow them to make a dignified exit, but what of the colleges that permit their standards to be lowered by youths who should be digging ditches or laying one brick upon another? Is it a question with the pundits of a handsome yearly budget, or of humorous indifference? In any case it is a disgrace.

Here is one humble suggestion. There must be hundreds of young men of the working class with alert ambitious minds who are forced to go out and toil at the earliest moment the law allows. Why not pass a law that would compel these college morons to exchange places with young proletarians eager for learning, the parents taxed to pay the tuition fees and 'keep'?

Why should precious education be wasted on those who are congenitally incapable of taking advantage of it, while young men as humbly born as Abraham Lincoln who, if properly equipped, might rise to positions of honor and usefulness are left to dig and dredge until ambition is dead, the higher faculties blunted, a fine citizen lost to the Nation?

We should relieve our colleges — and other institutions of learning — of their deadwood and plant live young trees in their place. The United States is supposed to be the land of opportunity. Here is another way to prove it.

In a more humble fashion certain of the 'little magazines' are bent upon giving the underdog a chance. Many young men and women, excluded from the regular magazines, are given an opportunity to make a name for themselves. It must be confessed that precious few of them have any talent for fiction. They are bright, write well, sometimes brilliantly, make deft character sketches and word pictures, work the stream of consciousness stunt for all it is worth. The majority are doomed to peter out, but at least they have been given a chance, and if these rather thin and anemic publications turn out two or three writers with an authentic gift for the story they will have justified their existence.

And the regular magazines will be the gainers in the end, as well as the few whose story-telling faculty was at first insufficiently developed to pass them through the sacred portals. Or were too original for editors wedded to the 'professional' story, sure to find favor with the great mass of middle-class minds. They might even replace some of the hack fictionists, which would be an unmitigated blessing.

But the weeding out and the helping hand to ambitious but impoverished youth should begin in the high schools and colleges.

CHAPTER XII

WHY HUMILITY?

HOW many of us are weary beyond words of hearing and reading that mouldy old *cliché* about our individual insignificance in this vast universe, that we are invisible dots in the immensity of space, our brief span in its relation to Time as meaningless as life on an ant hill? One of the most influential and thoroughly self-satisfied writers of our time, now dead, pretended to be an apostle of this creed, and preached it ad nauseaum. I had grave doubts of his sincerity.

Not long since, Doctor Edward M. Pallette of Los Angeles, in addressing twelve hundred leading physicians and surgeons at the opening of the California State Medical Association, made the following statement: 'With at least sixty per cent of its population intellectually adolescent, America is in danger of becoming a nation of subnormals.'

Quoting the correspondent who reported the address: 'To prevent such a catastrophe he urged laws requiring medical examination and other measures which would enforce sterilization before marriage upon those found eugenically unfit to be parents. He also advocated *that the right to vote be based upon intelligence test.* (Italics mine.)

'He took educators to task for spending too much time on the subnormal, or "underprivileged" child and suggested that instead they devote their attention to the normal and supernormal child, forcing no one to remain at school after the age of fourteen unless his or her grade was satisfactory. He also urged stricter immigration laws and propounded the rule of sacrifice of the individual for the good of the species in considering the problem of the care of the vast mass of incompetents.'

To quote Doctor Pallette direct: 'We not only support our ever increasing number of incompetents and give them without charge food, clothing, and the best of medical care, but we encourage them to have large families and permit them to choose, often from among themselves, the men who make our laws. We may be overwhelmed by the load of the defectives and incompetent among us and our civilization may go the way of all its predecessors.'

Well, I am willing to admit that these subnormals are invisible dots in the immensity of space, for, as I have remarked elsewhere, they are merely animals walking on two legs when they should be down on all fours. As far as this article is concerned they don't count except to throw the others into higher relief.

There are millions of intelligent beings who play a dignified and useful part in life, humble or important, and one and all possess a deep and abiding sense of individuality that would never have been implanted if the earth were an ant hill.

Every man (I use the term in its generic sense), even if deeply imbued with religious faith, is not only a lonely soul, but, however unaware, the centre of his universe. The world revolves about him; whatever his lack of awareness, this instinct is as deeply planted as the instinct of self-preservation. Others — perhaps the majority — are governed by this mighty Ego within them, and although such may acknowledge the worth of their fellows and the superiority of those who have risen to eminence and power, yet each to himself is of infinitely more importance. Even if science has made him a materialist, still instinct is greater than reason.

The devout will tell us this belief is born of faith in a blessed hereafter for which the present is but a test and an education; scientists who accept the doctrine of Herbert Spencer, that each intelligent being is a spark emanating from the great body of force behind the Universe, to which it will return in due course. To the complete materialist we are merely a chemical compound, but their attempts at explaining the life-spark, which before it left the body of a corpse made every human personality different from every other personality on the face of the globe, and animated the gray pulp of the brain with MIND, a metaphysical process that even X-rays have never brought out into the light — these gentlemen are as unconvincing as they are wordy and dull.

Certain it is that if that secret belief in one's supreme

individual importance were suddenly exorcised, mankind, without hope or interest, would revert to all fours, cities would topple to ruin, civilization would roll up like a scroll and leave not a memory behind it.

It is the I Am I, man's intense interest and belief in himself as an ego by divine right, that is the secret of all progress. What makes a civilization? A mass of individuals, and the mass is no greater than its parts. Every man with a functioning brain is as important as Life itself or he wouldn't be here at all.

Reading a recent book I was moved to wonder if this doctrine of individual insignificance did not originate in the thirteenth century. In my studies of ancient Greece and Rome I found no trace of it. Certainly neither Plato nor Aristotle had any such qualms — except, just possibly, when they realized the finite quality of knowledge. I doubt if it will be found in the works of Saint Augustine, one of the three great thinkers of antiquity.

The book in question is 'A Certain Young Man of Assisi,' by Mary E. Southworth, and privately printed by the J. H. Nash Press of San Francisco. It is the only life of any saint I ever read through, for it must be admitted that, however scholarly, most of them are hard going. But this book, the result of profound study and undoubtedly authentic, is so vividly dramatized and such 'easy reading' that it might have come from the hand of a practiced novelist.

The certain young man of course is Saint Francis, who develops from a roystering youth, the indulged son of a rich merchant who made night hideous for the good people of Assisi, into a being so holy that he was a saint before he had time to die and be canonized. He renounced not only the world but its barest comforts, preaching poverty and *humility* until it was a wonder there was any of the essence of personality left. But although he reduced his mind to an elemental simplicity he knew perfectly well what he wanted, and when he walked barefoot to Rome to obtain recognition for his Order he gained more concessions than he made.

Humble as he was, sweet, lovable, mystical, a saint on earth, the mule he was sometimes forced to ride was no more stubborn. The Church put a stop to the bare feet and rags that made him and his followers look like mendicants, and eventually herded them into monasteries, decently clad in brown robes and sandals; but long before that the Franciscan faith had spread far beyond Umbria, and today is the most numerous of all religious orders.

Many rich men at the very beginning renounced their wealth to join the brotherhood, and grew humbler and humbler.

There is no question that the Franciscans have proved a beneficence to the human race, and possibly human nature owes to them what unselfishness it may have developed throughout the centuries, but I do think the humility part has its drawbacks. I cherish the theory that out of the thirteenth century was born the inferiority complex, which, as I have suggested before, if it should overrun the earth would dry up the roots of civilization.

Fancy every man saying to himself, 'I am nothing. What's the use?' And meaning it. And never retracting.

On the other hand, we all of us know persons so maddeningly conceited we'd like to see the Franciscans have a chance at re-educating them.

CHAPTER XIII

UTOPIA

ONE of the more interesting claims of our enterprising chemists is that before long they will provide man with synthetic food. There indeed would be an answer to the unemployment riddle. If laboratories could turn out enormous quantities of 'food' reasonably cheap, nourishing, palatable, even taxpayers would cease to roar, and, could this dream come true, the need for new deals would vanish overnight. Also, we should hear no more dire prophecies of more and more millions to feed as new mechanical inventions reduce the need of man power.

We have had uncountable nostrums from economists, but not even birth-control can approach tabloid nutriment as a solution to a problem as old as life itself. And even were all of these nostrums to be adopted they would not do this generation any good.

In less civilized times people starved either through such blind stupidity at the top as finally precipitated a revolution, or because the inventive faculties of mankind were still undeveloped. Even today the greatest single menace certain nations have to deal with is overpopulation. Also today, we are so civilized, or sentimentalized, as to contend that merely because a man is born he has a right to live, no matter how useless.

Immense numbers of the human race, blind victims of indifferent Nature, are far less intelligent than dogs and cats; they are of no use in the world, add nothing, give nothing, and those who are of use work their brains dry or until their fingers ossify, and then die prematurely of heart disease, in order that the superfluous may live.

Well, so be it. Playing King Canute wastes time and invites apoplexy among the sentimentalists. The tide in favor of the incompetent is still rising and no man may push it back. Time may cause its recession, but not yet. The sentimentality of moderns is the strongest weapon in the hands of communists, and they know how to use it. One of their cleverest dodges is to affect sentimentality themselves, a weakness of which they are incapable.

It would be ironic if synthetic food should prove the irresistible foe of all isms. The Federal Government could lock its Treasury doors, give the overworked alphabet a permanent rest, and stock the land with synthetic food at little cost to itself. The economists would write no more futile books and even the birth-controllers would be mute. Families could increase to Biblical proportions, recalling the good old days when children on a farm were almost as plentiful as chickens and could be fed as cheaply.

The only question will be what to do with them all. It would be idle to confiscate the ranges of the West, for they are of little use for farming purposes and are needed for the more important cattle. Of course many small towns could be extended, but the spread might be so rapid that we should wake up some morning and find every square mile so densely populated that all an aviator could see would be one sprawling town in all the land. Senators and even representatives would lose their bearings, get their pork barrels mixed in Congress, and wistful references to the Old Home Town would be heard no more.

No, there is but one solution to the impending problem. Build up, up, up, instead of out. Rear tenements whose roofs would be lost in the clouds; also of synthetic, therefore cheap, materials. So, too, would be the furniture, habiliments, luxuries, including silk stockings and lipsticks. All shops on the top floor.

Little man, what then? One recalls the old lament: All dressed up and nowhere to go. Millions living in comfort without crooking an elbow; differentiated from those that work only by the dissimilarity between natural and synthetic food. Nothing to look forward to as too many are at work already, and, as the exceptions with brains and ambition would inevitably light out for themselves, the mental average remains low. Manna from heaven but nothing in the pocket. Amusements: television, the radio, inexpensive moving pictures, a canned orchestra in the vast room devoted to communal amusements, all provided by a canny government who will keep them as far off the ground as possible. Plenty of room for exercise on the roof.

Would they still be material for communists? Hardly. They are free and fed. And no bureaucracy to make them work. So strong is habit, they are happy in mere existence, for their education is rudimentary — wise government again — and their reading matter the lighter romances, a subject quite within their comprehension, for romance — to use a polite convertible term — is thoroughly understood in those buildings half a mile high and covering many acres of land and swarming with young people.

With plenty of time to think, if the euphemism may be applied to the average mentality of these comfortable human ants, discontent might blossom even in that stultifying atmosphere. But the Government thinks of everything. Without hope in this world the mature will be encouraged to pin their hopes on the next. Churches will lift their steeples closer to heaven than ever before, on the roofs, and well-paid resident preachers will paint in glowing colors the life to come.

Well... anyhow, it *would* be a solution. All hail to the Labs!

Since writing the above I have read of a neat Fascist plan to settle the Jewish question once and for all. So confidently does Adrian Arcand, the leader of the Canadian Fascist party, look forward to his ism sweeping the world that he has made definite plans for the disposal of the Jews. To quote from an interview with this optimistic gentleman: 'We will ship them off to Madagascar. The French and Polish Governments have investigated the island and according to their report it is capable of sustaining 110,000,000 people. We will not give it to them for nothing, of course; we will make them pay for it. Rothschild personally can pay $1,000,000,000.'

Now, why not get ahead of the Fascists and buy Madagascar for our increasingly superfluous population? Our Government is always on the alert for new ways of spending money, so what better use could it make of a few millions, and give permanent relief to our unfortunate taxpayers? Inspired with enthusiasm, I read up Madagascar in the Encyclopaedia Britannica, and assembled the following facts: It has a tropical climate but even and healthy. It is beautiful to look at and extremely fertile. It has rivers and lakes, lagoons and waterfalls. 'African humped cattle were introduced several years ago, and now exist in large herds all over the country. The fat-tailed sheep, goats, and swine have also been naturalized as well as all kinds of domestic poultry.'

Fish abound. The 'food-giving plants' are rice, maize, millet, manioc, yams, sweet potatoes, arrowroot. Numerous fruits and vegetables are of foreign introduction. The natives, of whom there are nearly three million, are friendly, lazy, and picturesque to look at.

An ideal existence for millions of Americans who are tired of looking for work, conditions that grow more and more uncertain, and who have given up all hope of that ancient ideal, 'security.'

And, come to think of it, why pour any more gold

into the greedy French coffers? Why not advise that recalcitrant Government that we are willing to take Madagascar in lieu of the war debt and call it a day? It should jump at the chance.

As for the Jews, they will always find a haven in enlightened countries, and are far too energetic for Madagascar.

CHAPTER XIV

SUPERWOMEN

LESS than half a century ago a woman was an 'old maid' at twenty-five, her matrimonial chances gone, no place in life for the derelict but attendance on an invalid parent or as a useful aunt; a mere shadow in the background of life. Only if she were a 'school-ma'am' did she survive in the community as a person of sorts.

Of course the psychological effect must have been deplorable. No matter how resigned (or noble), the canker of despair must have eaten at the roots of her being, for the end of hope is death in life. Metabolism slows down, the ductless glands secrete fewer and fewer hormones to race through the blood stream, the digestion suffers, possibly the heart. At thirty those women must have looked as old as a woman of sixty does today — that is to say, a woman of sixty who has 'let herself go.'

Today no one seems to care how old a woman is, after first youth has passed, and being married or spinster has little to do with her position in life. The term 'old maid' is as obsolete as 'lady novelist.' The unmarried woman may have a career in any one of the arts or professions, in journalism, politics:

mental decay unknown in any but the neurasthenics and the hopelessly flabby. Or, her metabolism races, the hormones dance in her blood stream, with the countless minor interests modern life provides for woman — not forgetting bridge! (Quite different, of course, in countries ruled by dictators, but then dictators don't last forever.)

This unique era of ours has been execrated as the Age of Speed, the Machine Age, the Prelude to Chaos, and what not. As a matter of fact it is the most interesting period in the world's history, and a Godsend to women.

I do not mean to say that women are happier, for happiness is too rare and fleeting to bother about anyhow; but if they are even moderately intelligent they can escape boredom, a condition which no longer should be the curse of the human race.

Moreover, for the first time in modern history they are comparatively independent of men. It is not so long ago that some man was the arbiter of every woman's destiny, and if no man at all dawned upon her horizon that was sheer tragedy. It is likely that every woman whose hormones are properly balanced would prefer a mate, and children, to travelling life's long journey alone; and the more intelligent they are the more satisfaction they get out of the companionship of men; but the point is, if they cannot find husbands life is full of other resources. They may regret, but they don't drift into backwaters, growing dimmer and older every moment.

And having travelled that far, the time has come

for the beginning, at least, of a race of superwomen. I do not believe that any but the most embittered would strive for a revival of the conditions in Egypt and other women's states in the fifth and preceding centuries B.C. No intelligent woman wants to be as superior to men as all that, for then she would forfeit her deepest, however secret, zest in life. If she holds to her common sense she will be more than satisfied with equality.

Aside from the unrivalled efficiency, to say nothing of success, women have achieved in so many ways, take the matter of looks versus age. Millions of alert 'modern' women know the psychological as well as the business value of keeping their 'looks.' When past middle age they have outgrown the folly of wanting to look 'young,' but they are determined to look *well;* in other words to laugh in the face of the years. In short, not to suggest the word age at all. Hence that thriving industry known as Beauty Salons, and the immense improvement in the average woman's dress.

But it is only the fools who imagine that external help alone can counteract the wear and tear of the years. The intelligent woman not only gives due heed to all that modern science has taught the world about diet, exercise, above all moderation in every sort of indulgence, but she watches the behavior of her organs and glands.

The reproductive glands, which supply so much motor power to the others, may in a measure be reactivated by the Steinach treatment, now so famous, but for those who cannot afford this recourse, or are prejudiced against it — there are plenty of old fogies left in the world and they exert their influence — the most important gland to watch is the thyroid (respectably situated in the neck).

Depleted energy in an enormous percentage of cases is owing to thyroid deficiency. More careers have come to an end from this lack than from preventable diseases. And no disability is so easily remedied. On the other hand, it should never be self-applied, for if the gland is still functioning to capacity (the exhaustion owing to some other cause), an increase of thyroid in the system may ravage the heart. It should never be taken except on a doctor's prescription after a basal metabolism test. But thyroid (taken daily, possibly, for the rest of their lives) will be a dominant factor in the increasing power of women, who may live to be a hundred, continue to 'look well,' and be as active mentally and physically as at forty. They will have an accumulated wisdom and experience that no young woman can hope to rival; the only fly in the ointment will be that they are likely to outlive their male contemporaries.

Life is harsher for men than for women, who seem to have developed a tougher fibre; moreover, men seldom can be induced to take the same care of themselves. Consequently their moral as well as their physical resistance wears thin.

I often feel sorry for men. How quaint that would have sounded fifty — even thirty — years ago!

CHAPTER XV

ESCAPE LITERATURE

(AND A FEW VERBAL SINNERS)

I

SOMETIME ago Charles Hansen Towne, in a moment of high exasperation, took both writers and public to task for their constant use of words that have no legitimate place in the language: *contacted*, *normalcy*, *react* (in its present adaptation), *camouflage*, were a few. And for working more lawful words like *meticulous* and *picturesque* to the bone, until they must feel like digging their own graves.

A pet vocable just now is *escape*. Once that comfortably established word meant nothing more significant than getting out of the way with all possible speed when danger threatened. From a house afire or a charging bull. 'He made good his escape' was once 'a ringing phrase.'

But words, until they die out of the language altogether, like *odzooks* for instance, must have now the same sense of insecurity that human beings experience when they have invested their money to the best advantage. They never know when they will be jerked down from their peg among the old stand-bys and bent to some new use that will make them weep (for words *have* life) until they grow accustomed and indifferent.

Escape has been made to dance to a new tune, and is particularly beloved of book critics; no doubt one of them, in a moment of inspiration — or desperation — lifted it off its peg, gazed at it lovingly as one would at any thought-saver, and started it off upon its devastating career.

The Literature of Escape! What a resounding phrase. How impressive, compelling. One might almost say, how blinding! No wonder it was taken up with passion. A slight ambiguity but added to its fascination; coming upon it for the first time the mere layman might reasonably wonder what it meant, and our old friend the Man from Mars assume at first glance that Literature, bored with too much attention from those who live by, off, and on it, had spread its wings and made for the stratosphere.

Or — and this seems more plausible to the M.F.M. — does it mean that the reading public has discovered that a certain kind of book is more interesting than another? More completely distracts the mind of the reader from depressions, life's monotonies, private sorrows, strikes, dire political portents, and the like? If so, then the Literature of Escape is a beneficence and should be canonized, not, as the astute M.F.M. soon discovers, used to convey a sneer, by the subtle manipulation of a once four-square word.

Ah, yes. He has hit the nail on its bromidic head. The Literature of Escape as a phrase (now a smug well-established *cliché*), is employed on a high derogatory note to condemn, even to outer darkness, the historical novel, the mystery and adventure story, the psychologically unusual; all fiction in fact that emanates from minds endowed with imagination — but never, oh never, applied to the novel or short story revelling in the small and repetitive details of daily lower-middle class or proletarian life, that depicts small people who never, not under the most miraculous change of conditions, could emerge as personalities in real life. All, all, that is blessedly commonplace.

Or heavy-handed novels about boiler factories, strikes, labor versus capital: whatever deals with mass production and the Machine Age; poor white trash in the South. Always — and estimably — authentic, but unrelieved by a gleam of inborn creative fire that might lift it into the realm of art — and, incidentally, make it interesting.

Now, Now, NOW, must be the watchword of the ambitious author who would win the approval of the literary pundits. What if certain historical novels, to say nothing of mystery stories, do attain sensational sales? All very well in their way, nice escape literature, but not IMPORTANT. Only the vital questions of the moment, especially those that arise from the ranks of labor, are worthy of serious pens. For nothing else *matters*. That they may be dated and forgotten a year hence while the work of imagination, particularly the historical novel written as no contemporary could possibly have written it, may endure for generations, never seems to occur to these gentlemen, ardent crusaders that they are.

Nor... that the more intelligent and intellectual type of writers and readers may be excrutiatingly bored with subjects that confront them from the front pages of newspapers, are mulled over in every review, serious magazine, weekly — never does that occur to our critics, who are not only conscientious but have the jitters every time they think they may have lost their place on the bandwagon by praising, in a bemused hour, some necromantic work of art.

But these lapses are few, and, conscientious creatures that they are, their concern is not so much for the reader as for those new writers of promise who may be beguiled — through lack of sales — from the strident NOW into the wake of those authors who seem — to our anxious critic — to be seeking an ignoble detachment: when, for instance, they spend a year or two upon some work of fiction that resurrects the great dead and brings to life the historic past. The emphasis of sneer on *escape* is far heavier when applied to the hard-working author than to the compliant reader, although he too is censured for reading only what interests him.

Well... I for one do not believe that the author of an historical novel finds any more escape than the sincere author of any sort of fiction. If the Nowist is worth the salt on his melon he becomes completely absorbed in his story of pots and pans, strikes, plush furniture, his machine-age revelations that smell of oil and sweat, his exaltation of labor, righteous indignation against capital. He is doing his best — unless a mere opportunist — to express himself, his aspirations, his hope of heaving the world out of its age-old rut; and, if he can accomplish it, to pour cold facts through the crucible of Art. Therefore, is he so utterly absorbed in his work that it is to him a complete escape (even from the facts he writes about!); it is his delight and his pride and his life apart.

The author of the historical novel, of course, is transported from the present both during his months of research and when re-creating a time long past, personalities whose very bones are dust. A fascinating game, but no more fascinating to one with that particular gift than the effort of his step-brother to make the Now so entertaining that the reader will canter along the highroad of Escape for a good three hours.

Nor does the writer in one genre tear his hair any oftener than the disciple of another. All creative writing is hard work and all creative writing is a delight. Therefore all *literature* offers the priceless boon of escape. When fiction fails in this vital respect then is it mere hackwork. The trouble is that the driven critics do not always differentiate between the two.

(I have said nothing of the many fine novels of contemporary life that occupy an exalted place midway between the novel of the past and the lower stratum of the present. Aside from the virtues that make them literature, they are good current history and will be valuable a hundred years hence to students of our times. But just now even they are somewhat out of favor because their mental distinction makes them seem almost frivolous to the proletarian enthusiasts. However, they are able to take care of themselves.)

2

And what of the other words that roused Mr. Towne's ire? They are but a few of those that elicit groans from his readers, his confrères — and consoeurs. I am no pedant. The genius of a nation is often expressed in its slang, and every writer should strive to add a word to the language, else how will language grow? But it must be a word for which there is a definite need and place; just as the War, the cinema, aviation, have made substantial and inevitable contributions.

But that is vastly different from such ungrammatical hybrids as *contacted*, a word that induces in me every time I hear it the same murderous impulse as when someone asks me, 'How did you *react* to that play (or whatever)'? The immoral conversion of the noun *contact* into a verb no doubt started in the business world, where it saves time — at least the tenth of a second, and this is the age of speed. But there is no excuse for its adoption beyond those fevered hordes, for it is not only bad grammar but a word that fairly grates on the eardrum, a word, moreover, that has an indefinable air of vulgarity, which *almost* drops it into the class of *folks*, our pet American vulgarism.

As for *react*, one cannot quarrel with Dr. Freud for giving it a new meaning, for, in their entire vocabulary, psychoanalysts have found no one word so useful; but in that particular interpretation it should have found no place in ordinary conversation. It took root however during that brief period when it was naïvely believed to be highbrow to prattle about the Oedipus complex and psychoanalysis in general, and was freely adopted by persons with poverty-stricken vocabularies.

Obligate is another frequent sinner, used, incredibly, by otherwise impeccable writers. It throws the best-wrought sentence out of balance, just as Paul Robeson in 'Show Boat' was too big for the scenery.

The English *will* say 'partially' for 'partly,' 'speciality' for 'specialty.' It is useless to argue with them; but perhaps they might renounce 'those sort of things' if they would, just once, transpose that phrase to read 'things of those sort.' They are no more careless than we are in their use of 'liable' with the verb, nor in combining none, nobody, somebody, someone, anybody, everybody, with the plural pronoun. I read not long since in an English novel of definite pretensions: 'None of the men wanted to be alone in their cabins.' There are times when it is almost obligatory to use one of these locutions in order to avoid pedantry, but not often, and the effect on the eardrum is as irritating as a split infinitive — or 'neither... or.'

'Like' for 'as,' once the hallmark of the illiterate, is running neck and neck with 'react' and 'contacted.' *Normalcy* was one of the very worst counts against President Harding. Not only is it a flabby word but there was no excuse for it whatever. Normality was and is a perfectly good word.

Enthuse, reminisce, suspicioned, suicided, transpired (for happened) are but a few of the vulgarities of American speech that would fill a column of the tallest newspaper. Ah, yes — lest we forget: 'drapes,' a Westernism worthy to rank with 'meet the wife.'

No one could do so much to restore and preserve the purity of the English language as radio announcers, but there are too few that do not rasp the ear with voice and accent, to say nothing of commonplace sentences and mispronunciations. However — if they do not say Ottomobile and Iceolation, we are grateful, to so resigned a pass have we come. Some day we may have a tsar who will muster all but three or four out and replace them with educated and accomplished men whose incomes have suffered from depressions.

3

A word may be said here about verbal misbehavior.

Why is it, I wonder, that so many of the younger writers, particularly the Leftists, are in one respect so reactionary? Subjects, words, phrases that for at least three quarters of a century have been tabu in literature besmirch the pages of authors who might otherwise be read with profit and pleasure.

The proletarian fictionists are by no means the only sinners. Other young writers who aspire above all things to be MODERN seem to regard certain verbal misbehaviorisms as the very latest evolution of the unfettered mind. Even some of the older ones occasionally fall into a panic and make a leap for the band-wagon. Observe Maugham for instance, one of the most distinguished writers living. Every once in a while he seems to say to himself: 'Strewth! I must roll down from the heights and wallow for a minute or they'll be calling me one of the old boys.' And forthwith interpolates any irrelevant obscenity he can think of. And he so capable of making his points without dipping into hogwash!

For these verbal insults to literature are as sure a sign of imaginative paucity as to use death arbitrarily as a climax; death is always strong and another good old reliable. So may impudicity be relied upon to make the reader, who otherwise might find the story rather thin, sit up and gasp; also continue.

But is it modern? Quite the contrary. It reads like old Fielding and Smollett, minus the robustness and plus a smirking self-consciousness of which the eighteenth century was innocent. It is old-fashioned, reactionary, the desperate resource of authors who write fiction not by the grace of God but by main strength. When the established writers succumb in moments of panic, or cool calculation, they have less excuse, for they have long since learned how to write with power and point, and they also know all about antiquated cultures. Hemingway, of course, is a striking case of infantilism. Without that feeble spot in his brain and with more imagination he might have made a place for himself in literature.

It is another matter with the Latins. Reticence is no virtue of theirs. But why, having improved upon our old bad habits, should we return to the trough? No one has asked women to revert to black cotton stockings and high buttoned boots.

Surely each generation should travel far ahead of the last, travel along the road of progress, not run back to sniff at old dung heaps.

4

To return to the stimulating Mr. Towne. He once wrote an article in which he expressed the wish 'that someone would create a word to describe the kind of person who uses grandiloquent phrases when simple ones would do so much better.'

I recalled that I had invented the word 'sophisticate,' which had been taken up generally, and felt the stirring of ambition. Why not invent another? After several hours of mental convulsions I emitted 'bathosticates,' rejecting 'orotunds' and 'rodomants,' which may be found in Roget's Thesaurus. At least everyone knows the meaning of bathos, so why send a harassed people to the dictionary? But although I delivered the word in print it was not received with favor, possibly because it is one of the ugliest words ever coined, however apt.

But whether we have a word for it or not, the irritating fact remains. With very few exceptions — two of them are Henry James and George Meredith — the first-rate authors, no matter how extensive their vocabularies, have always expressed themselves lucidly, and with a certain distinguished simplicity —

Froude and Jowett, for instance — that is as far removed from the commonplace as Lazarus was from Dives. Both James and Meredith were stylists, but often maddening to the reader. The gods endowed Henry with genius, and he could afford to tie himself up into hard knots, for if not generally popular he had and still has a passionate following; but writers with neither genius nor a high order of talent had better watch out.

Of course all ambitious authors should constantly enlarge their vocabularies, emulating Shakspere, who is said to have commanded sixteen thousand words; the sin lies not in using unfamiliar words, as Harold Nicolson so often does, but in what Mr. Towne so aptly calls grandiloquent ones.

It is to the credit of the younger generation of writers that one rarely finds them striving for merely verbal effects. They are shamelessly downright and terse. It is among the more mature as well as the elder crop of authors — and 'conversationalists' — that we find the direct descendants of those Victorians who were careful to say 'limbs' when they didn't mean arms, and were accused of putting panties on piano legs.

Out of this daintiness grew the habit of discarding the simple word in favor of the more 'imposing'; of roaming round and round the mulberry bush instead of coming directly to the point; above all, of sentimentalizing the language. The radio fairly drips with sickly phrases. And heaven knows most of our political orators could qualify as bathosticates; for *bathos* is not only a caricature of *pathos* but embraces every kind of balderdash. Socially we hear less and less of it, although some left-overs who fancy themselves as conversationalists are inclined, if encouraged, to be puffy and snuffy and guffy.

The more old-fashioned writers, at least, could not do better than to read Maugham's 'The Summing Up.'

CHAPTER XVI

NO MORE BEAUTIES

WHEN I was about twenty and living in Atherton, then known as Fair Oaks, two of my sisters-in-law took me to call on Mrs. Sanderson, wife of the eminent Judge, who had rented a house for the summer in Menlo Park. This was a yearly custom that bored me excruciatingly, for all of these important ladies who dared to invade the sacred faubourg of Menlo Park were twice my age — even my two elder sisters-in-law, as I have mentioned elsewhere, were but a few years younger than my mother — and took as little interest in me as I in them. But I was a resident, a young matron living in a house of her own, and 'the family' saw to it that I performed my social duties. So, when the summons came, I threw aside my experimental pen, dressed myself in white lawn with a black velvet belt and a black band about the throat, a leghorn hat with a heavy blue veil to protect my complexion, thick chamois gloves to shelter my precious hands, and stepped rather sulkily into the char-à-banc when it arrived.

I had no premonition that I was about to meet a girl who not only became the most interesting friend I ever had but one of the two most famous prima donnas of her day. Nor did the spirit of prophecy descend upon me when I met her on this occasion.

We were sitting in the long cool drawing-room, the older women gossiping and I ignored and bored as usual, when a girl entered and went over to Mrs. Sanderson, addressed her in a low tone, and taking no notice of us. A short rather fat girl with a heavy homely face not even redeemed by the fresh complexion of youth.

'My daughter Sibyl,' said Mrs. Sanderson perfunctorily, and the girl nodded with no graciousness whatever but mumbled into an impatient ear. I looked at her with complete indifference. Heaven knew I longed for a young person to relieve my boredom, but the hiatus between twenty and forty is a mere earthquake crack to the abyss between twenty and fifteen. If she had come over and sat beside me I should have called upon all my politeness to avoid looking as superior as I felt.

It was four years before I saw Sibyl Sanderson again. Her mother took her to Paris and left her there to finish her education. I forgot about her until she returned to San Francisco, made her début in Society, and immediately became 'the rage.'

I did not happen to go to town that winter, and, alone in my woods with no neighbors to furnish me with the latest gossip, I barely heard of her. But when everyone returned for the summer I heard of little else. She was a beauty. Very *very* Parisian. Such clothes. Her figure. Her style. All the men were mad about her, and there were 'stories.'

I had never seen the metamorphosis of an ugly

duckling into a beauty, and I was not only astonished, but as a potential author, aside from being a female, I was vastly *intriguée* — a verbal pet of the moment.

I remembered that large heavy face, half hidden, it was true, by a sun hat, that fat body; and while I knew that any girl's figure might change between fifteen and nineteen, it was incomprehensible to me that anything short of a miracle could have remodelled those features.

She spent the summer at the fashionable Hotel Del Monte, and I saw her for the first time at a large ball the following winter. I was standing with a group of friends between dances when one of them exclaimed: 'Sibyl! Look! Look! You haven't seen her yet.'

I turned my head. A girl was walking slowly toward us attended by three cavaliers. 'Sibyl Sanderson?' I asked. I could see no resemblance to the utterly commonplace creature who had wandered in and out of that drawing-room in Menlo Park.

'Yes! Yes! Isn't she stunning?' Stunning was the word of words.

She assuredly was. She carried her head high, her body with an easy grace that made her look tall whether she were or not. Her figure, with its small low bust, sloping shoulders, delicately curved hips, slender tapering arms, the rest of the body encased in a skin-tight black velvet gown 'cut very low' was unsurpassed by any I have ever seen. Her beautiful neck and shoulders may have been plastered with the whitewash then in vogue with the more daring, but her white complexion with its dash of red was too

clear for artifice. Her appearance was the more startling, however, because 'no decent woman' in those days
made up (a little powder was the very limit), and her
shining dark hair was indubitably reddened, her long
eyelashes were thick with mascara, and if her cheeks
were not painted her lips were.

But I was more interested in her features, for, as I
remembered her, she had none worthy of the name.

Well, her mouth was large, her nose negligible, the
lower part of her face still heavy. But her eyes! I
recalled the hat with the turned-down brim and realized that I had not caught even a glimpse of her eyes:
she had not condescended to raise them when introduced.

They were magnificent. Large, blue-gray, luminous,
and although her manner was languid, almost to the
point of insolence, they expressed all things as she
slowly moved them from one to the other of the
besotted faces hanging over her. Perhaps it was owing
to the mascara, I thought, trying to be charitable,
but they looked to me more like the eyes of experience
than what one was accustomed to in a girl of nineteen.

'Looks fast, doesn't she?' said one of my friends.
'The way she rolls up her eyes is a caution to rats,'
another expressed herself in the choice slang of the
moment. 'Her idea is to look like a French cocotte,'
explained a third. 'It is the fashion of those ladies of
the Lower Ten to wear tightly fitting black broad-
cloth on the street, very severe, with no relief but a
bunch of violets, and you never see Sibyl out-of-doors
in anything else.' The men with us said nothing.

I saw her two or three times quite close that night, and noticed that although when she was not talking her large face was heavy and expressionless, the moment her eyes lit up the whole countenance was transformed. But even in repose she had more personality than anyone in the room.

I was immensely interested and determined to know her. A few days later I called in the usual formal manner, and she happened to be alone. We became friends at once.

Her manners were natural and charming, she had a keen sense not only of humor but of fun; and, serious and often tragic as she was in later years, the best back-stage comedian I ever met. In this and subsequent interviews, particularly when she spent a day with me now and then in Fair Oaks, she explained among other things the phenomenon of her transformation from a homely cucumberish schoolgirl into a beauty, and one whose magnetism was equally potent. (The term 'sex appeal' was unborn, but magnetism served in our more limited vocabulary.)

After she had been at a fashionable boarding-school in Paris for a year and 'learned a few things,' she took herself in hand. 'I knew I couldn't ever be a real beauty,' she said with her devastating frankness, 'but I could make people think I was. I can walk into a room full of the prettiest women in town and make them look like nothing.'

She cultivated the 'beauty air': that mien of serene confidence in one's irresistible charm, unmarred by conceit, as well as what the French call *autorité* —

both projecting an almost audible command for homage, masculine in particular.

Banting was the word for dieting in those days, and as her superb figure developed she conquered the natural greediness of youth, gave attention to 'carriage,' poise, grace, studied all her 'points,' and collaborated with her dressmakers later on. She modelled her manner, her style, on the famous cocottes, the French aristocrats being too dowdy for her taste. There is little beauty in Frenchwomen of any class, and not their face but their style was the fortune of the demi-mondaines (among other things). They could be seen and studied at the races, on the stage, in the Bois, on the street, holding themselves with an air, and looking as if they trod the apex of the world. A liberal education for a keen-witted girl determined not to look like a thousand and one other American women turned out by Worth or some other highly respectable Paris 'milliner.'

Sibyl soon discovered that a kindly Fate had endowed her with a magnetic fascination, and she cultivated subtlety and charm of manner. Her knowledge of men was partly instinctive, and she learned more from all available sources. It amused her to return to respectable San Francisco looking like everything she was not and give it a succession of electric shocks; too secure in the social position of her family to fear ostracism from the fogiest.

I soon discovered that she was as bored as I was. She found the San Francisco men 'children' after the Europeans she had met. Most of them had to be put in their place. Few knew enough to play up to her. Being a demi-vierge was no cinch.

We also had a bond in common in our private ambitions. I wanted to be a writer and the very word horrified my demi-Spanish in-laws, while as for my husband he raved every time I had an article in the *Argonaut*. Sibyl had a lovely light lyric voice and yearned to be a prima donna, but Judge Sanderson had 'put his foot down.' But I have told all this in my autobiography, and have brought Sibyl into this chapter as an example of how a woman may be beautiful when she is not. I will add however that although I have seen a good many comparatively plain women transform themselves so cleverly as to appear pretty or even beautiful at times, I think in Sibyl's case there was one determining factor lacking in the others: an inflexible, determined, ruthless will. Charming as she was, kind, generous, loyal, she was wholly selfish at the core, and would have sacrificed her nearest and dearest to accomplish her ends.

Fortunately most women are not so constituted, and comparatively few are motivated by an ambition to outshine at all costs. If they are animated with a desire to improve their appearance, the result if effective is as gratifying to those that have to look at them. And if they excite envy in others that may inspire a determination to do likewise. And the more the better!

Many wait until they begin to go off. But in others vanity, one of the most natural, and useful, of human frailties, develops early. After all, what is vanity but a form of aspiration, a vague subconscious desire for perfection? It stems from the same root as progress, without which we should still be living in caves and eating roots and raw meat. And with more of it we should have fewer middle-aged and elderly women who look like shopworn remainders and are an offence to the eye.

I doubt if anyone was ever vainer than I, but I certainly was not unique, for what I am about to relate was no doubt typical of thousands of vain young females, else a book called Ugly Girl Papers would not have been written, nor outsold the most popular novel.

I was in my early twenties when this book came out and I bought it at once. So far, my only concern had been to protect my complexion and hands and give my hair twenty strokes at night. Although by no means wholly displeased with my appearance, I was far from satisfied. If I could have waved a wand I should have had Spanish black hair and dark green eyes with phenomenal lashes. Well, for miracles I could not hope, but who knew what hints that book might give me? 'Ugly Girl Papers.' I certainly was not ugly, but if I followed advice given to those less fortunate it was just possible I might turn out a raving beauty. And beauty in those days was rated above riches, genius, fame, 'living happily ever after.'

One of the admonitions in this fascinating work was to take a thorough steaming once a week, a simple rite that could be performed in one's own bathroom. Explicit directions were given. I bought a large glass spirit lamp and a bottle of alcohol, but concluded to try this beneficence first on one of my younger in-laws who was afflicted with many freckles. She required some persuasion, for it sounded rather daring, and to the Athertons even powder was anathema. I vowed secrecy and one morning she drove over alone in her phaeton to my house, where all was in readiness. Under a cane-seated chair was a large wash-basin, and in its middle the new spirit lamp under a small pan of water. She exchanged her clothes for one of my nightgowns (a concession to modesty), I seated her in the chair, wrapped about her a heavy blanket that covered not only her person but the chair and the basin, and she looked like a well-swathed mummy with a slightly alarmed face resting on the upper fold of the envelope. Then I knelt down, lifted a corner of the blanket, and lighted the lamp. The water bubbled merrily. She began to perspire freely and I almost fancied I could see the freckles roll off her face.

I was regarding my handiwork with rapt attention. The alarm had receded from her eyes, her rather pasty skin had attained the hue of a ripe tomato, we were exchanging congratulations, when, without a warning hiss, there was a loud report, the fierce crackling of glass, the low roar of angry flames. My beautiful spirit lamp had blow up.

I was terrified to my marrow. Her state of mind may be imagined, for not only were her arms pinioned but the blanket held her fast to the chair. The basin must be full of burning alcohol; in another moment the flames would dart through the seat of the chair.

We screamed in chorus. I clawed frantically at the blanket, and found myself unwinding it the wrong way. But I had it reversed in a second, and pitched it into the bathtub. My victim gave a leap, dashed into the bedroom and into her clothes, and out of the house. It was some time before I saw her again. Nor did I try that particular renovator on myself.

But nothing daunted, I tried others. I had a clear white skin, but there were, despite all my precautions, at least three freckles on the bridge of my nose and they caused me acute distress. Either in 'Ugly Girl Papers' or elsewhere I read of Perry's Freckle Lotion, and I bought a bottle and duly anointed myself. It removed the freckles but it also removed the skin, and my nose was red and swollen for a week. As nothing would have induced me to admit my vanity I secluded myself and made my husband, from whom it was impossible to hide the secret of my affliction, tell everyone I had a bad case of poison oak. I think the Family had doubts, for I had often rubbed the leaves of that wicked vine between my hands to show my immunity. They may have been the more suspicious for, taking a hint from the U.G.P., I had appeared one day with darkened eyebrows, and, despite sarcastic remarks, continued the habit; I was tired of being one of Nature's own blondes and thought the time had come for a highlight.

I next turned my attention to my hair. It was pale gold and received an occasional compliment, but I thought it insipid and longed for a bronze or copper tint. I read that lye was very improving to colorless hair and ordered my Chinese cook to get some and make a strong concoction. Fortunately Chinese have little curiosity and he did as he was bid and then went to his room to enjoy his afternoon opium pipe. The nurse was out in the woods. I gave my hair a thorough shampoo in the harmless-looking liquid, and retired for siesta. When I awoke I ran to the mirror full of eagerness and hope. I should hold my head an inch higher if my crowning glory resembled the beautiful copper boiler in the kitchen.

Oh, horror of horrors! My hair was bright scarlet. My very personality seemed changed. I looked ten years older. I made a wild dive for the kitchen, and the imperturbable Chinese made another strong concoction, this time of washing soda. Once more I shampooed. The soda bleached off the red but left my hair as colorless as tow, harsh, brittle. It was several weeks before my poor hair resumed its natural tint and quality.

Alas, that the road to perfection should be sown with thorns! After that I let my hair and complexion alone save for the cold cream with which I plastered my face at night, but my figure still worried me. I was excessively thin and longed passionately for a bust. That is odd reading these days, but there *was* an era when no woman could have a 'figure' unless she boasted the proper mammiform development.

Then as now I was a light eater, but I forced myself to consume the rich Spanish dishes my husband delighted in, to say nothing of sweets. Useless. No plank was flatter than I.

Then one day my eye lit upon an advertisement in the San Francisco morning newspaper. Thin ladies who desired a beautifully rounded bust might call at a certain address on California Street and receive valuable advice and a jar of cream, which, made from a secret and infallible recipe, would cause the very soul of the woman who used it to rejoice, or words to that effect.

I discovered an ailing tooth and took the train for the city on the following morning. California Street then as now was one of the principal arteries of San Francisco, and I had no difficulty in finding the address; observing casually that although the entrance was on one street the house on the high terrace was on the corner of another and faced Saint Mary's Cathedral.

I climbed a flight of covered steps, rounded the terrace, and rang the bell of a small nice-looking house. The door was opened by the benefactress herself, and she led me into a simply furnished parlor and made me feel completely at home. She was a large kindly matron with a soft pleasant voice and dressed severely but smartly in black. I was much impressed.

She finally produced a large jar of cream for which she demanded an exorbitant price, but I paid it without flinching, so great was the confidence with which she inspired me, and being an optimist by nature.

When I left, instead of making at once for the stair, I wandered to the edge of the terrace and stood there for several minutes, gazing north on the side street into the famous Chinatown, then up and down California Street with its new cable cars in which I might catch a glimpse of some friend; everybody used those cable cars, that led from downtown through the fashionable district, until the automobile was invented; the steep hills were hard on horses and long détours necessary.

I looked up at the immense and hideous mansions of the new bonanza and railroad kings that were causing so much comment, then sighed and walked slowly to the steps that led down to the street. How I should have liked to live in San Francisco instead of spending an occasional winter there with my mother-in-law, and how I hated the country! I have hated it ever since except in small doses.

There was nothing to do but get my lunch at Swain's, a *very* respectable family restaurant where I was permitted to go alone, and then return to my woods. Fair Oaks was merely a collection of country houses, and although it had a way station all trains did not stop there. George, my husband, met me at Menlo Park, and as we drove home I confessed my morning pilgrimage, knowing I would let it out anyhow. As a rule he was mildly amused at my attempts to beautify myself, but as I went on to describe the location and my wanderings on the terrace, he gave the reins such a jerk that the mare — a beast with wicked ears that I detested — stood on her hind legs and nearly bolted.

'My God!' he shouted. 'Do you know where you have been? California Street, indeed! That house is on the corner of Dupont — the worst street in town and that house you were in is notorious. Dupont Street! ! ! (I nearly fell out of the cart. Of course I knew all about that foul street. Who didn't?) There isn't a house in it outside of Chinatown that is not —— ' Here his language became altogether too descriptive for print. 'If you had wandered down a block — and it's a wonder you didn't — you would have seen painted women soliciting behind half-open shutters. They would have hurled at you the vilest epithets they could think of, and any man passing would have had the right to insult you. Why, oh, why, am I married to such a little idiot? Anyone, *anyone* may have seen you from a passing car! You and your damn bust! And I'll bet that stuff is no good. She knew she could charge you what you were fool enough to pay, for you wouldn't dare to go back.'

Usually I replied to any animadversions on his part with spirit, but this time I was too subdued and frightened to 'talk back.' Dupont Street! Moreover, my faith in myself as 'a judge of human nature' was severely shaken. If ever a woman had looked respect-able... and so kind and nice.

I was prepared for the worst, but fate was amiable. No one had seen me. The Family lived and died in blissful ignorance that one of their name had spent half an hour in a house of prostitution hobnobbing with a madam. Of course the cream with its secret and infallible ingredients was worthless. There was nothing to do but yield to the importunities of my dressmaker, and pad. And at least I had my complex-ion.

Complexion. A word one seldom hears in these days, when veils and even parasols are out of date and girls and young married women (to say nothing of fat and middle-aged horrors) vie with one another in acquiring a summer hide unrivalled by darkest India. But at that time and for many years after no one could be an authentic beauty unless Nature had given her a faultless skin, blonde or brunette. Lily Langtry was as famous for her radiant complexion as for her lovely features, her faultless figure, her grand air. Mrs. James Brown Potter, a delicately tinted brunette, was a society beauty before she went on the stage. To pick names at random from the past without regard for chronology, Nance O'Neil, Lillian Russell, Emma Eames, Maxine Elliot, Marcia Van Dresser, Ethel Barrymore, Sibyl Sanderson (la belle Sibylle, they called her in Paris); Geraldine Farrar, Mary Garden — all these famous women would have been independent of make-up if footlights had permitted.

The equally famous beauties of England's aristocracy had the clear white skins of the north, with natural color in cheeks and lips: the Duchess of Leinster, probably the most beautiful woman in the world during her short life; Princess Henry of Pless (Daisy Cornwallis-West), who looked like a fairy princess, and was the daughter of Mrs. Langtry's only rival; Lady Colin Campbell, who had a skin like polished ivory; Lady Warwick and her sister the Duchess of Sutherland. All these women had features cut by centuries of breeding, regally poised heads, figure, grace, but if they had been sunburned or freckled or coarse-grained of skin they never would have been admitted into that sacrosanct circle of professional beauties, nor painted by academicians and hung on the line at the yearly exhibitions of the National Academy. Even the Queen's young granddaughter, Princess Alixe of Hesse, afterward Tsarina, was as stared at for her rose-leaf complexion as for her fine profile and discontented expression.

Of course it was more natural to have a perfect complexion in Britain than elsewhere owing to the fogs, but, aside from those Americans already mentioned, there were many in our cities who had fresh and natural complexions and were proclaimed as beauties in the society pages of the newspapers. In New York, Katherine Duer Mackey, Mrs. Philip Lydig, Mrs. Burke-Roche, Mrs. John Jacob Astor, afterward Lady Ribblesdale, Mrs. August Belmont. All of these superb-looking women could be seen in their boxes at the annual Horse Show, or in the once-famous 'horseshoe' of the Metropolitan Opera House. In San Francisco we had Mrs. William Crocker and her niece Elsie Sperry, whose dash of Indian blood gave them a peculiar distinction, Mrs. Rudolf Spreckels, Aileen Ivers, Mary Belle Gwynne (Mrs. Kenneth Kingsbury), whom the late James D. Phelan, a connoisseur, called 'the most beautiful girl of her generation,' Ruth Holliday, Jeannie Selby, who married my brother-in-law, Faxon Atherton, and at an earlier date Alejandra Atherton until she put on too many Spanish pounds. And then there was Amélie Rives of Virginia, whose novel, 'The Quick or the Dead,' made such a sensation in the eighties, and owed its success as much to the young author's exploited beauty as to its emotional content. No publisher thinks of playing up an author's beauty today.

Why is it that one never hears of great beauties any more? On the stage, on the screen, in society? Not even in England, where beauty in private life was first given a market value: literally, for photographs of professional beauties, as exclusive socially as the Queen, were on sale in the shops.

Even Helen Wills, who might have posed for Praxiteles, or be Pallas Athené reborn, would never have received more than passing mention as a beauty had she not made a world reputation as Queen of Tennis. Her classic features were merely incidental in the public mind; a pleasing accessory, nothing more.

The absence of dazzling complexions — sacrificed to the actinic rays of the sun — the moving pictures that attracted thousands of pretty girls of all classes to the various meccas and made beauty a drug on the market, the reorientation of women in general by even the echoes of the long campaign for political equality, the increasing demand of a public that has grown up for personality and talent on both stage and screen rather than mere looks — all of these are contributing factors, no doubt, but I think that above all credit must be given to the ubiquitous beauty parlor (or 'salon'). It is too easy to be pretty, handsome, even beautiful, these days. Women, long resigned to being plain, discovered that rouge and lipstick, artistically applied, massage, dull lank hair tinted and waved by an expert, not only transformed their appearance but induced a psychological permutation that drove Time to cover. They held themselves with more confidence, took a definite interest in dress, in hygiene; a new sparkle dwelt in their eyes.

Before the advent of the beauty salon women stumbled along that thorn-sown upward grade, inspired by a desire for improvement, as best they could. I remember — sometime in the nineties it must have been — asking at a fashionable New York drugstore for the latest thing in cold cream. The clerk produced a jar and told me importantly that it was used by two well-known 'authoresses.' 'Those old things,' I said, elevating my youthful nose. 'How absurd!' 'Yes,' he replied deprecatingly, 'but they like to look nice.'

Quite. And when I met them later I realized how much worse they would have looked if they had neglected their skin altogether.

A natural evolution of the beauty salon was the cosmetic surgeon who restored the contours of the face: a Godsend to women of the stage. I know of several who were enabled to go on acting young leads long after the time when other actresses of their age were resigned to middle-aged rôles. A few years earlier their only recourse would have been massage, which, practised to excess, loosens both skin and muscles. Some even pulled the sagging skin up under low waves of hair and fastened it to the scalp with court-plaster.

Later followed the Steinach reactivation treatment,

which bucked up the endocrine constitution and enabled women in all fields of endeavor to hold their own against younger rivals.

A wonderful age we live in.

And all very well — but beauty, authentic beauty, has it departed never to return? There is not a woman in the world today famous for beauty alone. Even in England, where they still have fogs and features, the term 'professional beauty' is as extinct as the autocracy of kings. The most perfect complexion is overlaid with make-up; make-up is the fashion, and Fashion is a tyrannical goddess. In Hollywood the actresses whose reputations are world-wide, even when they have a fair amount of looks, are in no wise comparable to the beauties of the past. Excessively pretty, many of them, striking, 'personalities'; but if a really great beauty did apply and could not act, or had no box office IT, she would find herself relegated to the ranks of extras, or advised to go home and find a husband.

In a way this is a cultural ascent, like anything else that demonstrates a higher degree of intelligence in the public; and as for the women in private life, or those whose improved appearance enables them to earn a living with fewer rebuffs, one can only feel that progress is climbing. Grateful that thousands of women have a renewed hope and pleasure in life. Wishful only that more would follow their example, that there were fewer middle-aged and elderly women whose vanity it is to have no vanity and look like old wrecks cast up by the sea. Often rich women at that.

As far as we know the worship of beauty originated in ancient Greece. Perfection of form was attained by youths in gymnasia, but the admiration of female beauty was expressed in statues of Pallas Athena, Ariadne, Aphrodite, Artemis, Hebe, Chloris, Calliope; the same goddesses chiselled later by the Romans under Latin names. And down through the ages the worship of beauty in woman has been a part of the world's history until now.

(It is true that the ideal of beauty may have changed from time to time. Either that, or fascination, seductiveness, some trick of expression, have given certain women of history a reputation for beauty belied by their presentments in marble or on canvas. I once at a private view in Paris saw an original portrait of Diane de Poitiers. She had butter-colored hair slicked back from a knobby brow, eyes so heavy they seemed falling from their sockets, a correspondingly sensual mouth, an inconsequential nose, and a pasty skin. I found her repulsive — but, for all I know, even a modern man might not. Certainly, although ten years older than Henry II, she ruled him and France until his death, while the lawful Catherine of the Medicis secreted more and more poison in her system and bided her time. Diane reigned as Queen of Beauty as well as unofficial Queen of France, and even inspired the statue by Jean Goujon — his masterpiece — that stands in the Louvre. She must have had a blinding fascination!)

Of course it may be argued that with thousands of beauty parlors, expensive and cheap, running at high speed, the cult of beauty is more pronounced than ever. That nine out of ten women are 'beauty-conscious' (even more so than I in my twenties). That the average is higher than ever before. That practically every woman on the screen is charming to look at. That a girl in any walk of life must have misshapen features to remain ugly. And even these may be remodelled by a plastic surgeon. Cosmetics will do the rest.

Quite true. But too much of anything lowers its value. Like bread and potatoes it is taken as a matter of course. (Trite, but ever true.)

When Lily Langtry, far back in the eighties, made her début in London Society men stood on chairs to look at her over the heads of intervening crowds. Other crowds followed her on the street. Nor were these passionate admirers in the same class with the silly little geese who fight for autographs of Hollywood celebrities. The Jersey Lily in her youth had the exalting beauty of a goddess, and the intelligent public gazed upon her with something of the awe and rapture with which they listened to great music or impassioned oratory.

And so it was with other professional beauties of that time. Men, both in England and the United States, used to cluster about the doors of churches waiting for the loveliest of her sex to emerge and give them a gracious smile. Audiences sometimes rose in the theatre when a surpassingly beautiful woman entered her box. In Hyde Park both men and women stood on the hard little chairs they had rented for a penny, to see the objects of current worship drive by: extremely aloof, exquisite of profile and complexion, the personification of a national ideal.

No more. No more.

The public may run after celebrities today, but not because they ache to gaze upon beauty — as a lover of music might ache to hear the Ninth Symphony; certainly not because they worship it. Pretty painted faces are as common as legs, which, to paraphrase the London bus driver, ain't no treat to nobody.

Something has gone out of the world; one dimension, perhaps. One source of inspiration at least. One spur to idealism. With the passing of beauty worship — natural authentic sovereign beauty — the esthetic standard of life is definitely lowered. The natural correlative instinct of the herd is to equalize everything. Universal standardization — hateful word — exaltation of the average.

A man who had the Christ complex said to me once with genuine indignation, 'No woman has a *right* to be more beautiful than a thousand others who are just as good as she is: just as no one has a *right* to genius or fame that exalts him above his fellow-creatures.' He wasn't a communist either, merely a crusader in the cause of justice and fairness and equality whose intelligence had run a little to seed.

If he had lived a few years longer he might have looked toward a future that bid fair to realize his ideals in a way; possibly, unless his mind cracked altogether, a certain uneasiness might have begun to stir within him.

Let us make a violent effort and imagine that war has devastated every state in Europe. That fanatics have deliberately razed the magnificent cathedrals heretofore spared during centuries of warfare, or cunningly restored. Cathedrals that have drawn hundreds of thousands of travellers from every part of the world to gaze with awe and reverence and enrich their memories. The châteaux of France to which artists dedicated their God-given genius. The romantic castles of Germany. The monuments, Gothic in particular, of the Middle Ages. The severe beauty in marble and stone of the Renaissance. The Alhambra of Spain. The sacred ruins of Greece and Italy. The Vatican … all the famous galleries of painting and sculpture. The mellow old castles and baronial mansions of Britain, her cathedrals of historic memories. Windsor Castle. The Tower of London. Her thousand 'corners' beloved of pilgrims. All, all gone. Their very site forgotten.

And in their place? Well — communism has run its course. Common sense now prevails. Common sense, now regarded as human nature's proudest attribute. Prosperity has ebbed back. Where the accretions of the ages had stood, picturesque, romantic, uplifting, each stone emanating a whisper from the Past, are now millions and millions of houses, some larger than others but all alike; very pretty, very sanitary, very comfortable, but all alike. Public buildings more severe of outline but by no means ugly, and extremely adequate. All alike. All standardized. The expression of a good average intelligence.

The imagination faints after such a prolonged strain — but it might be.

Would any one of spirit, high intelligence, mental or spiritual aspiration, want to live in such a world? I doubt it. Nevertheless, it looks as if we were headed that way. Indifference to beauty in women may herald indifference to beauty in all forms, the death of the esthetic sense. There may not even be a cult of ugliness — of which there are spasmodic symptoms at present — merely of the commonplace.

Let us draw the veil and hope the United States will continue to remain neutral.

CHAPTER XVII
ONE OF THE MYTHS

Lytton STRACHEY shattered the Florence Nightingale myth, and we know now that far from being a saint on earth, an angel of light, she was one of the most ruthless creatures that ever lived, as hard-boiled as a big business man, used the very life blood of public men to accomplish her purpose.

Fortunately her purpose was a great one, she was as high-minded as she was hard-boiled, destiny was on her side, and she was distinctly the most useful woman of her time. A slip of Fortune's wheel that would have projected her into life on one of its lower planes, a disorder in her glandular system, and one shudders to think of the evil she could have accomplished in the world before being hanged at Tyburn.

A great woman gone right, but no mere angel with a lamp.

There have been other historical myths, lasting for centuries, to be demolished finally by some mind more inquiring and thorough than its fellows. Aspasia is a case in point. Owing to the slanders of the comic poets, the yellow journalists of their day, who hated Pericles and sought to harrow him in his most vulnerable spot, she was branded as a hetaera or courtesan by historians during the revival of interest in the almost forgotten glory of Athens; gentlemen who no doubt found the slanders of Aristophanes and his crew more spicy than the unmistakable attitude of Plato and Xenophon. As a matter of fact she was what today would be a morganatic wife; as a 'foreigner' she was unable to marry Pericles legally, owing to an unfortunate law he had sponsored. So far as is known she had no other lover and lived with Pericles as his respected wife (by all but the comic poets) until his death. She was a wealthy girl who came from Miletus with the architect Hippodamus for the sake of its larger intellectual life. No need for her to enter the ranks of the hetaerae, women who had cultivated their minds that they might be kept in luxury by brilliant men whose wives were uneducated and who preferred the converse of other men, to say nothing of their propensity to worship the beauty of youths trained to perfection of grace and form in gymnasia. Clever women beyond the pale sought to rival both, and often succeeded. If a wealthy heiress had invaded their exclusive circle they would probably have scratched her eyes out. (I have written something of this in another of these chapters, but it cannot be too often emphasized.)

But although this indisputable fact was demonstrated in 'The Immortal Marriage,' and authorities quoted from whose profound researches there is no appeal, she is still grouped with 'the famous courtesans of history' by superficial writers. Time-honored legends die hard.

One of the historic myths that will indulge in the longest period of expiring kicks is that which persists in attributing the downfall of Spain to the expulsion of the Jews in the fifteenth century. William Thomas Walsh's 'Isabella of Spain, the Last Crusader,' was published in 1930, and in the years that have passed since then must have found a wide circle of intelligent readers. His list of authorities at the end numbers nearly a hundred. In that work, both authentic and fascinating, he demonstrates beyond further debate that the Jews were as innocent as unborn lambkins of the shrinking of Spain from a world power into an insignificant peninsula somewhere down in the southwest of Europe.

Nor need any inquiring mind have waited for the publication of 'Isabella of Spain.' The facts, if one looks below the surface of mere words, may be found in any encyclopedia.

This myth should have exploded long ago, certainly since the publication of Walsh's book. But it has not. Influential columnists and magazine writers, orators indulging in rolling periods, still, no doubt in all innocence — or ignorance — reiterate that old tarradiddle; and, for all we know, the teachers of history in schools may not have opened their minds to the facts but send forth pupils primed with one more item of misinformation. Since Hitler has indulged in his malicious — or possibly politic — persecution of the Jews, he has probably been warned twenty thousand times of what the expulsion of the Jews did to Spain, particularly if he reads the American newspapers.

Well, the expulsion of the Jews had nothing whatever to do with the eventual downfall of Spain, and here are the facts.

In the fourteenth century the Black Death ravaged Europe, and it is estimated by historians that half the population succumbed. As the Jews had always been hated for their religion, their arrogance, their extraordinary facility in making money, and their intellectual gifts which enabled them to coruscate in the arts, sciences, and professions, there more than once had been futile efforts to extinguish them. The Black Death gave the godly an excuse for massacre on the grand scale. Some sincerely believed the Jews had poisoned the wells, or had practised black magic; and if, in that age of ignorance and superstition, a few here and there noted that the Jews too were perishing by millions, they chose to disregard mere facts and joined the mass persecution. Pope Clement VI, a humane and enlightened man, thundered in vain.

In Spain the Jews had numbered four million eight hundred thousand. The plague disposed of two million. In June, 1391, forty thousand were massacred by Christian mobs. Extermination or flight faced the rest, for even the several governments of Spain as well as the clergy seemed willing to accept the picturesque theory that twenty-five million Europeans owed their hideous death to the sinister machinations of the sons of Judea.

The influence, wealth and power of the Jews in Spain had steadily increased since the beginning of the eighth century. By the fourteenth practically all the wealth and commerce was in their hands, and although they were hated by the masses for their uncanny magnetism for gold, for their unconcealed arrogance, and the ostentation in which they lived, they were protected by the kings and nobility; as money-lenders they were extremely useful at a pinch.

The massacre of June, 1391, gave them a terrible jolt. That deep-mouthed roar of religious hatred, growing more ominous every moment, cracked the foundations of their self-confidence. Their quick intelligence forbade any further self-delusion. There was but one way out of the dilemma and they took it. Two and a half million of those spared by the plague were baptized into the Christian faith. They became known as Conversos — New Christians — and the title passed on to their children. When Ferdinand and Isabella ascended their respective thrones and joined forces in matrimony there were but few more than two hundred thousand professing Jews in Spain, and they, with perhaps two or three hundred exceptions, were segregated in the Juderia, poor and miserable for the most part, of no influence whatever in the state.

Not so the Conversos. They were wealthier and more powerful than ever, for many had married into the families of grandees, and social prestige abetted their in no wise weakened determination to control the finances and commerce of the country. In addition they now held many of the most important posts in the governments of Aragon and Castile.

Nor was this all. Conversos were Christians, whatever their blood, and therefore eligible to priestly office. 'They mounted the hierarchy so quickly,' writes Mr. Walsh, 'that in Isabella's reign an impressive number of the bishops were of Jewish descent. Every church, every chapter, every monastery, had influential connections; and in some dioceses Jews directed the ecclesiastical revenues.' Cardinals, bishops, archbishops, ministers of state, bankers of the realm, dictators of finance, dictators of industry. Once more it looked as if they might form a state within a state, less visible than the New Jerusalem they had contemplated a century before, but infinitely more dangerous.

And they would have been as safe as the 'Old Christians' themselves but for one thing.

Moberly Bell, the editor of the London *Times*, once told me that so strong was the soil of Egypt that if one planted American cotton in that country it shed its native properties underground and rose to the surface as Egyptian as the hands that tended it. So it must have been with the religion of the Jews, that reached back into Biblical antiquity, and beside which Christianity was an upstart, a mushroom, a mere evolution from Roman paganism, which the Jews had respected as little.

These Conversos gave lip service to the Catholic Church. They attended Mass in state on Sunday, confessed, took part in pageants, observed Lent, contributed heavily to the ecclesiastical exchequer when called upon. On Saturdays they attended the synagogues, cooked with oil instead of lard or fat, except when entertaining Old Christians, and ate unleavened bread during the Jewish holidays.

At first they were extremely wary and their secret allegiance was unsuspected. But as the years passed and the Conversos were, beyond all question, the most powerful body of men in the peninsula, the wealthiest, the most enterprising, they grew bolder, and ever more arrogant. In the latter part of the fifteenth century they must have been allied by marriage with two thirds of the Christian families of Spain, noble and middle class. What cared they what any one thought of them? The time came when they indulged in open blasphemy.

Well, the religious instincts of the House of Judah may be indestructible, but the Christian religion had now attained the respectable age of nearly fifteen hundred years and it was the religion of the civilized world. Kings knelt at the throne of its Pope, architects dedicated their genius to its glorification, and no palace of kings could rival those cathedrals in splendor. The hierarchy was recruited from the noblest families in Europe, and men of the highest intelligence renounced the temporal world for the spiritual, and incidentally increased the authority of Romanism by their abilities and their ambition.

The roots of Christianity if shorter than those of Judaism were quite as tenacious, and in the masses there was a fine capacity for fanaticism. As the Conversos grew more careless, more arrogant, the masses in Spain began to seethe. Every corruption in the Church was laid to those of Jewish origin who had taken the vows; no voice was raised to remind them that clerical discipline had broken down in other countries where no Jews had entered the priesthood, and were few and unimportant without.

Isabella, Queen of Castile, and Ferdinand, King of Aragon, were married in October, 1459, seventy-eight years after the Black Death massacre of the Jews, and when the mighty Conversos were making a joke of the confessional and washing off the heads of their children after baptism in the cathedral. Facts or inventions? Who can tell?

Pressure was brought to bear upon Isabella to punish or expel the Conversos from the day she mounted the throne, for the Conversos were more aggressive in Castile than elsewhere in Spain. But although no more devout Catholic has ever lived, and no sovereign ever had a cannier respect for public opinion, it was long before she could make up her mind to act. She was closely allied with many Conversos. Her most intimate friend was married to one. Her confessor was of Jewish descent. To quote Mr. Walsh: 'Almost all her Privy Councillors and Secretaries had Jewish blood on one side or the other, or both.' And Ferdinand? 'His *escribano de racion*, a sort of treasurer, was descended from the Jewish Rabbi Azarias Zinello. . . . King Ferdinand's government, in fact, was virtually in the hands of Conversos. His chief treasurer, his confidential friend and adviser, his cup-bearer, his steward, all were of the seed of Abraham. It would have been strange if these shrewd and powerful politicians had not made every effort to dissuade the King and Queen from the step they were contemplating.'

It was owing to this powerful influence as well as

to the trouble in which they were still involved with Portugal that the Inquisition was delayed for eleven years after the two sovereigns had united their kingdoms. But they were far-sighted. In 1478 the Spanish Ambassador in Rome did, with some truth and more exaggeration, induce Pope Sixtus IV to issue a bull permitting the sovereigns to 'extirpate this dangerous sect root and branch from out your kingdom.' Furthermore, he permitted them to name the inquisitors, for he had been persuaded by the wily Ambassador that the Inquisition was but a temporary 'war measure during a crusade.' This cherished crusade of Isabella was to reconquer the entire peninsula, and only the Moors and the Conversos stood in her path. One of the most damaging accusations against the Conversos was that they were intriguing with the Moors to conquer all Spain and drive out the Christians or enslave them.

The awful word HERESY, however, had more influence with the Pope than aught else. No doubt had been left in his mind that one and all of those Conversos who had been received into the true faith had recanted, and blasphemously practised their abominable religion in secret. Burn, or force them to recant again before they poisoned the souls of the true Christians with whom they associated.

This bull, an imposing sheet of parchment with a leaden seal hung on strands of colored silk, was locked in a chest by Isabella to await the imperative moment for publication, and if its existence was suspected few had actual knowledge of the ominous step taken by

Pope Sixtus. Undoubtedly Conversos in high places had wind of it, but they relied upon their influence with the sovereigns and could afford to laugh.

They laughed until a Turkish fleet suddenly descended upon the Italian port Otranto and utterly destroyed it. Nowhere was the panic greater than in Spain, for the Moors were also Mohammedans, and who could predict what might happen if the Turks came to their support?

And were not the Conversos the secret allies of those infidels, whose capital was the wealthiest and most beautiful in Spain? Were not armies even now being trained for the conquest of Granada, their ranks full of Conversos who might betray Spain on the battlefield? To say nothing of the Conversos in high office? This time public opinion was too strong for Isabella, even had she wished to disregard it, but it must be said for her that she published the bull of Pope Sixtus as much to avert another massacre and 'protect faithful Christians among the Conversos from unjust suspicion and persecution,' as to rid Spain of her internal enemies and use their confiscated wealth for the holy crusade against the Moors.

The populace calmed itself. The Inquisition would extirpate the heretics root and branch, and what was a massacre compared with the exquisite satisfaction of gloating over thousands of Conversos burning at the stake? Moreover, the Turks had gone home.

The Inquisition opened in Seville. Many of the Conversos fled and took refuge in the country with friends among the Old Christians, but were brought back and forced to stand trial. The first auto da fé was held on February 6, 1481. The trial took place in the Cathedral after a solemn Mass. The majority of those arraigned confessed their errors, received their penances, and were reconciled to the Church. Six men and women were escorted by a civil guard beyond the walls to the Tampo de Tablada and burned at the stake, resisting the passionate appeals of the Dominican friars to repent and be saved. Several days later a few others shared their fate.

But the public was cheated of the enjoyment it had anticipated, for the plague had broken out and people cowered in their houses, afraid to venture into the streets.

'In the gloomy damp dungeons of the Fortress of Triana across the river, lay some of the richest and most influential men and women of Seville. The early Spanish Inquisition was one of the few persecutions in history in which the victims were chiefly millionaires, and the common people applauded.'

But they were brought forth to repent if they would, and during these first autos da fé seven hundred confessed, were reconciled to the Church, and marched as penitents in great processions. It is possible that the masses would have refused to believe in these new conversions and resorted to violence, but all their attention was centred upon a more personal danger. The plague was raging, and in Seville alone fifteen thousand perished during the summer. For the time being the Inquisition was forgotten. In the exodus from the stricken city many Conversos were able to escape, and took refuge in Portugal and Italy. Their properties were confiscated.

In 1483 the Pope, by this time convinced that the Holy Office was being used far more for political ends than in the sacred name of the Catholic Church, appointed Torquemada Inquisitor General, with instructions that no one should be burned for any offence but heresy. During the administration of this severe but conscientious man one hundred thousand Conversos were placed on trial and two thousand executed. It is not to be imagined that the Conversos submitted to the persecution and the heavy fines that amounted almost to confiscation without a mighty protest. But for the dramatic details of their conspiracies and punishments I refer the reader to 'Isabella of Spain.' This chapter does not aspire to be a history of the Inquisition, but to prove a point.

That equally great historic event, the expulsion of the Jews from Spain, those that called themselves Conversos and those that did not, took place in 1492. It was a step long contemplated, but might never have taken place had it not been for a sensational trial after which two Jews and six Conversos (of a low social grade) were condemned for crucifying a Christian boy on Good Friday, 'somewhat in the same way and with such enmity and cruelty as his ancestors had crucified Our Redeemer Jesus Christ, mocking and spitting upon him and giving him many blows and other wounds to scorn and ridicule our Holy Catholic Faith.' This, after examining the principal offender, who confessed without torture.

The plague was long since over. The conquest of Granada had been achieved. The populace were free to excite themselves over the Jews and Conversos once more. There were still wealthy Jews and even rabbis in certain of the Spanish cities, and how they had escaped the Inquisition it is hard to understand. Probably because they had avoided the Christians and had had no opportunity to Judaize them. The horrible revelations of this trial, of which I have given but a hint, so enraged the people that they roared for mass vengeance. Ferdinand and Isabella agreed with Torquemada that the only way to avoid a massacre like that of 1391 was to expel all Jews who refused conversion and all Conversos who were still under suspicion.

A number of important baptisms took place, but for the most part the rich Jews paid the travelling expenses of the poor of their race that they might not be tempted to renounce their ancient faith.

All — unrecanting or suspected Conversos, rich Jews, poor Jews, were given three months to put their affairs in order before the exodus, then left Spain unmolested by the masses, who, having attained their object, were quite willing to let the enemy go in peace. The number of these exiles? For many years it was greatly exaggerated, but the best authorities now agree that one hundred and sixty thousand were at this time banished from Spain. Some eight thousand had escaped during the early years of the Inquisition.

Now we come to the point.

Between August, 1492, the date of the expulsion,

and the destruction of Philip II's 'Invincible Armada' in 1588, ninety-six years elapsed, a period that might have been called Spain's Century of Progress, for she rose to an eminence and a power undreamed of in her past.

Ferdinand and Isabella, whatever their private sorrows and disappointments, had a glorious reign. Columbus presented them with a vast territory in the New World, and savages were being converted to the true faith willy-nilly. Spain, rid of all internal dissensions, flourished as seldom before. Wealth poured into her coffers. To quote Mr. Walsh: 'Andalusia was a blossoming garden. Castile was producing abundant crops of corn and wheat. The great glass works of Barcelona rivalled those of Venice. The silk industries of Seville were employing as many as one hundred and thirty thousand men. Fine woollens from the looms of Castile were exported to all parts of Europe. The leather trade was flourishing. Granada made velvets too fine to be imitated. Toledo wove carpets. Every city was like a great singing workshop.' Ferdinand conquered the Spanish half of Navarre, and recovered Roussillon from the French King, Charles VIII.

To the encouragement of the Queen Spain owed her sudden burst of intellectual, artistic, and scientific energy. The University of Salamanca, long closed, was revived, to become in due course the greatest of its time. The University of Alcalá, other universities, many schools, were built and flourished. Scholars came from all over the civilized world to increase their knowledge at these founts of learning. Medicine and other sciences made their most notable gains. Few events were more momentous than the birth of archeology, which in Spain was practically simultaneous with its first gropings in Italy. The studies of botany and zoology were ardently pursued.

As for literature, the Manriques were dead, but there must have been poets of fleeting celebrity besides the great Garcilasso to inspire Erasmus to write several years later: 'The Spaniards have attained such eminence in literature that they not only excite the admiration of the most polished nations of Europe, but likewise serve as their models.'

And this was before the full flowering of the Golden Age, of which Garcilasso was the forerunner, for Erasmus died in 1536.

Isabella, who took an active interest in everything, and was tireless in her efforts not only to make Spain illustrious among nations, but to improve its every condition, 'took measures to stop the deforestation that had produced bleak areas of treeless deserts.... And,' concludes Mr. Walsh, 'planned a broader progress, which if followed by her successors, would have eliminated one of the causes of the later economic decline.'

But alas, there is such a thing as too much zeal by benevolent despots, and Ferdinand and Isabella — Isabella more particularly, as the King was away with his armies for a great part of the time — in their encouragement of industry went too far. To quote from another authority. 'The State undertook to develop the herds of merino sheep by issuing prohibitions against inclosures, which proved the ruin of agriculture; and gave premiums for large merchant ships, which ruined the owners of small merchant vessels and reduced the merchant navy of Spain to a handful of galleons. *Tasas* (fixed prices) were placed on everything. The weaver, the fuller, the armorer, the potter, the shoemaker, were told how to do their work. All this did not bear its full fruit during the reign of Isabella and Ferdinand, but by the end of the sixteenth century it had reduced Spain to a state of Byzantine regulation in which every kind of work was under the eye, and subject to the interference, of a vast swarm of government officials, all ill paid, and often not paid, all corrupt. All this did not bear its full fruit until later times, but by the seventeenth century it had made Spain one of the two most beggarly nations of Europe — the other being Portugal.'

These were but two of the causes that contributed to the eventual downfall of Spain. There were more to come. But meanwhile, to quote Mr. Walsh again, 'Never were the industries and the commerce of Spain so prosperous, never was order so well maintained at home and prestige abroad, as during the sixteenth century, when Spain became the head of a new Empire that overshadowed all Europe and the Americas.'

And the Jews and Conversos who had laid the foundations for all this prosperity? How was it that the Spaniards got along so well without them? It may be proved conclusively enough to satisfy all but the most pig-headed that the Great Expulsion did not affect the fortunes of Spain one way or another, but I think there is one point that has been overlooked.

Quite aside from the fact that a respectable number of Conversos and rich Jews had convinced Torquemada and the sovereigns of their sincere conversion, and remained, so far as we know, good Christians — certainly not insolent and arrogant as of yore — the exiles had left *rivers of Jewish blood behind them*, coursing through the veins of thousands of the best families of Spain, families that would always be known as Old Christians. All that was bad in Jewish influence had gone, all that was good remained to enrich Spain with its vigor, versatility, enterprise, genius for finance, commerce, and the arts. One sees few Spaniards even today who show no trace physiognomically of Jewish ancestry.

No doubt these active, wary, far-sighted men protested against the regimenting of industry by the sovereigns, but were unheeded. Isabella, with whom Ferdinand knew better than to interfere, was a lady accustomed to having her own way; what she believed to be right was right and that was the end of it.

Ferdinand became known as one of the ablest rulers and diplomatists of his time. He died in 1516, surviving Isabella by twelve years. His son had died and he was succeeded by his grandson, Charles of Hapsburg, under whose reign (as the Emperor Charles) Cortez conquered Mexico, and Pizarro still further enlarged the American possessions, already immense, with the subjugation of Peru.

When Philip II ascended the throne in 1556 he found himself reigning sovereign not only of Spain proper, but of the whole of South America and a large part of North America, as well as of possessions in Central America and the Indies. Of the Aragonese inheritance in Italy, Naples, Sicily. Of the Burgundian inheritance — the Netherlands and Franche Comté, and of the Duchy of Milan. A vastly greater Spain than was ever dreamed of when the Jews were driven out in 1492, sixty-five years earlier.

But although Philip did his best, genius had been left out of him and luck was no friend of his. If he inherited the greatest empire in the world, he also inherited wars and enmities and entanglements that led to more. The economic legacy left to him by his illustrious great-grandparents reduced his internal revenues, and despite the gold that came now and again from the New World he was generally at his wit's end to raise money for wars in the Netherlands, to maintain his position as champion of the Catholic Church against the sturdy Dutch Protestants; for his wars with France and the Mohammedans, and finally with England.

How he ever raised the immense sums to build and equip the Armada for the 'undoing of England' is one of those mysteries so often encountered in history past and present when nations go to war practically on a shoestring. But accomplish it he did, and it sailed magnificently from every port to an ignominious defeat, administered not by Elizabeth and Drake but by Nature, who, not approving of the enterprise, whipped up a wild winter's storm in summer, and that was the end of the Invincible Armada.

Poor Philip struggled along for another ten years, and left an exhausted country, and warfare both active and pending, to his son. From these wars that proved so costly in both men and money Spain never fully recovered. And her possessions fell away one by one. Even the inherited Jewish blood was defeated by Circumstance and the follies and extravagancies of kings. Even if it had occurred to Philip III or Philip IV to recall all the descendants of the exiled Jews it is doubtful if they could have rehabilitated a country so exhausted within and without. It is still more doubtful if the Jews would have accepted the invitation, for they were busily engaged in adding to the wealth of the Netherlands and of England, far too prosperous themselves to make sacrifice for a country whose very name to them was synonymous with persecution, writhings and shriekings at the stake, a humiliating exodus.

But there is no reason whatever to believe that even if Conversos and Jews had been permitted to remain unmolested in Spain the history of that country would have read differently. There was enough Jewish blood left in the state to save it, but what could it avail against the short-sighted policies, the incompetence, the senseless wars, the extravagancies of kings?

Paradoxically, as Spain declined politically she immortalized herself intellectually and artistically. The three reigns that succeeded that of Philip II were known as the Golden Age of Art and Letters. Cervantes, Calderon, Lope de la Vega, Velasquez, Murillo. The University of Salamanca was famous all over Europe as the Spanish Athens, and ambitious scholars of all nations still haunted those Dominican cloisters. It is doubtful if they noted the putrefaction without.

Will not some genealogist trace the blood stream of Cervantes, Calderon, de la Vega, Velasquez, Murillo, back to the fifteenth century and ascertain how many Jewish corpuscles still vitalized the roots of their being?

CHAPTER XVIII
'THE WONDER
RACE'

I

IN 1927 a remarkable book was published in England by G. E. Altree Coley called 'The Wonder Race.' [1] Whether it excited any controversy in England at the time or whether it was published in the United States I do not know. I do not even remember how it came into my possession; possibly I saw an allusion to it somewhere, the title attracted me, and I sent for it. At all events, being hospitable to new ideas, it interested me and I never forgot it. The other day I read it again, and it seemed to me worth while to present an abstract of it and let others judge whether it is rooted in sound historical fact, however remote, or is wholly fantastic. That it is based on an interesting theory no one will deny.

The author begins by saying, 'It is strange that the most extraordinary phenomenon of the age should be accepted as a matter of course, without exciting the slightest curiosity in the general mind as to how it

[1] The Covenant Publishing Company, Ltd., London, England.

came into existence. The development of the Anglo-Saxon race from an obscure people living in a cluster of thinly populated islands into the great Empire with its great kindred Republic that together dominate the world today, is absolutely without parallel in the history of mankind, yet the historian and the scientist, quite as much as the ordinary person, simply assume that it "just growed." It is true the various details have received investigation. Historians have endeavored to trace the beginnings of representative government, or of colonial and trade expansion; but the race itself, its unique character, and the astounding series of fortunate developments which, dovetailing one into the other with extraordinary fitness, have given the race the dominating position that it occupies today — the phenomenon in its wholeness, in short, has never seemed to challenge inquiry.... Somehow it *happened* that Great Britain acquired the half of North America, and India, and Australia, and South Africa, and so on.... Nor again when he (the average citizen of the Empire) turns his thoughts back to his island history, does it strike him as wonderful that for nearly a thousand years it has been immune from foreign invasion.... Neither does it seem anything but natural that after an open-door policy that flooded the United States with immigrants from every country in Europe, the Anglo-Saxon race has remained on top to guide and control the whole by its inborn genius for liberal government and has not been swept under in a chaos of mixed nationalities ... the United States being wholly Anglo-Saxon in origin, laws, and language, and, more than all, in its general mode of thought, or what may be called racial instincts.

'Studying then the leading features of the Anglo-Saxon race we are first met with the enormous and unprecedented extent of territory that it dominates. ... The United States covers an area of 3,570,000 square miles. ... The British Empire, according to the *Times* "Atlas of the World," covers an area of 13,730,000 square miles, and includes a far more bewildering diversity of details, from Canada to the Malay Peninsula, and from the idyllic West Indies to the enormous reaches of territory in Africa ... Canada, South Africa, Australia, New Zealand, India, Rhodesia, Soudan, Kenya Colony, Mesopotamia, Newfoundland, British Guiana, the West Indies (the greater number), part of Borneo, New Guinea, and innumerable smaller but important places such as Gibraltar, Malta, Arden, and Singapore. But since we must add the United States and her colonial possessions as part of the heritage of the race, this results in the conclusion that the Anglo-Saxon race controls more than one-third of the land surfaces of the globe.'

After pointing out that Spain, France, Portugal, and Holland ('The Dutch, not the English, first colonized South Africa. Dutch navigators, not English, first discovered Australia, New Zealand, and Tasmania') each had the chance to gobble up the greater part of the earth's surface, but petered out, the author makes light of the ethnologists who aver there is no such thing as race, and even those 'educated Anglo-Saxons themselves who aver that the Anglo-Saxon race is merely a blanket term for what is not actually a distinct race but a mixture of races. They assert that in fact it is a mongrel race. This is certainly strange. International politics daily assumes there is such a thing as definite races in Eastern Europe, where a succession of peoples have in turn invaded and swept backwards and forwards from the dawn of history to modern times, yet it is denied to a people who for a thousand years have been interbreeding within the confines of their island home. And here it happens we find science on our side. While, according to the system of skull measurements that have been extensively applied to the various countries of Europe, there are wide variations to be found in each continental country, there is a striking uniformity of skull measurements in Great Britain, which we may take to indicate homogeneity of race. This supports Huxley's statement that racially the people of the British Isles are one, and both confirm the findings of the greatest historians. Celt and Dane, Anglo-Saxon and Norman are racially one.'

After discussing the widely differing mentalities of the various European and Asiatic races, each definite enough, the author continues:

'What then are the qualities of the Anglo-Saxon mind which make it differ from other racial minds? ... We may first select that one which will most readily be recognized as racially typical — the Anglo-Saxon genius for self-government. This strangely persistent faculty is to be traced throughout the history of the race and manifests itself in every offshoot as it colonizes different parts of the world. Through the ages it meets with many ups and downs, but, tenacious of life, persistently grows stronger and stronger. This political sense is the product of two interacting principles that are apparently contradictory — an innate love of liberty and innate loyalty. Dominated by the first quality men wrestle with their kings over the Great Charter, the Petition of Right, or the Stamp Act; guided by the second they willingly acknowledge the rights of others, extending the powers of self-government even among races that have been subdued by them....

'Love of liberty, it is true, is nothing uncommon, nor is it especially admirable.... It connotes a proud independence of outward control, that, as in the early history of England, may be morally disastrous. But loyalty is essentially ethical. It looks not on its own things but on the things of others.... The balance between liberty and loyalty can only be maintained by an innate and abiding sense of justice. And it will be recognized, in confirmation of this, that justice is a quality which the Anglo-Saxon race is acknowledged to possess to the extent, we may venture to say, of a racial characteristic.

'But whence springs this conspicuous and inborn sense of justice that is the foundation and safeguard of self-government? Whence this passion for liberty, this reverence for loyalty? Notice that they are all instinctive qualities. No amount of teaching can inspire the slave-hearted with a love of liberty to which he will sacrifice life itself. These are racial products. . . . We may well ask, then, can we find any circumstances in the history of the race that will account for these racial characteristics? Whether this is possible or not, of one thing we can be sure — that we must look for such an origin in a far more remote past than we are accustomed to associate with the Anglo-Saxon race, and for this reason: *that from the moment we first meet with it in history these very qualities are characteristic of it.*'

(We are getting there by degrees.)

'Now mark carefully. The development of the race first in the British Isles and latterly in the great expansion throughout the world is not the result of any definite plan so far as any great man or any council of men could have planned it. . . . Bishop Stubbs says: "The march of constitutional progress is so steady and definite as to suggest everywhere the idea that it was guided by some great creative genius or some great distinctive tradition. Yet it is scarcely ever possible to distinguish the creative genius, it is impossible to assign the work to any single mind or series of minds." . . . Again and again the historians have recourse to the expression "it happened!" Times without number the student is forced to see that had it not been for a fortunate combination of circumstances, over which the actors could have had no possible control, failure and miserable disaster might have been the record. . . .

'We have already seen how "it happened" that the Conqueror made a change in the law of feudalism that robbed it of its greatest power for oppression, and how "it happened" that England possessed a principle of equality in law of all ranks of society save the kings and his barons-in-chief that contributed inestimably to her social and political advancement, and which was unknown on the continent. Actually it is in such constitutional developments that we find the strongest evidence of that design that attains its ends through all ups and downs, and by the aid of fortunate accidents moves onward in spite of the frequent stupidity, stubbornness, or even desperate opposition of the actors.... There is a fact that is true of the Anglo-Saxon race that is true of no other in the world.... The English have had their full share of military exploits, yet no one seems to find it unusual that none of those exploits has been enacted in driving out a foe that has fastened itself upon the country; and no one finds it strange that the various menaces of invasion have been one and all turned aside, so that since the addition of the Normans to the race Great Britain has enjoyed nearly nine hundred years of immunity from any invasion from an enemy; or if, as we rightly conclude, the Danes as well as the Normans were but branches of the same race claiming their share of the island together with the Angles and other early comers, we may say that England has never been subjected to the ravages of a foreign enemy.'

After giving a graphic summary of the 'spirit of discord' that ravaged practically every state in Europe, invaded again and again, the author once more calls attention to the fact of England's mysterious immunity: 'Even the most casual reader of history cannot fail to ascribe ultimately the defeat of all attempted attacks to a series of fortunate occurrences which some call good luck and others call the hand of Providence.'

The most dramatic of these 'happenings' was unquestionably the destruction of the Spanish Armada by a providential storm. Spain at that time ruled the world. Her Armada was 'invincible.' England with her inadequate navy would not have stood a chance if forced into conflict. The Spanish hordes would have swept over England, Protestants would have been subjected to all the ingenious tortures of the Inquisition, the pride and hopes of England would have been extinguished. But — 'It was then that strange intervention of the forces of Nature once more fought against the enemies of England. In the summer month of August the most fearful of gales swept down from the North Sea and drove them northward up the coast of Scotland past the Orkneys and the inhospitable coast of Ireland, sinking ship after ship on the way, sinking them with the fetters and instruments of the Inquisition that were meant to torture the limbs of free and protestant England.'

(During a critical moment of the World War William Jennings Bryan said to me: 'I wonder if Providence will intervene with a miracle to save England as it did in the case of the destruction of the Spanish Armada?' He had not read this book, of course, but as that is one of the 'miracles' that stand out in history, it was hardly necessary.)

'It happened' that Mary, wife of Philip, died

without leaving a son. 'It happened' that Philip, aided by France, was foiled in another attempt at the conquest of England. Mutual bickerings between the two forces prevented this design upon 'the stronghold of the Reformation' until England possessed a powerful navy of her own and it was thought wise to leave the heretics to their fate. 'It happened' that Mary of Scotland had no issue when married to the young King of France. 'According to established custom had there been a son from this marriage he would have united Scotland with France, and, since Mary stood in undisputed succession next to Elizabeth, this would have meant the union of England as well. Nor was it necessary to suppose that the looked-for union must await the death of Elizabeth, for her claim was regarded by many as inferior, from the circumstances of her birth, to that of Mary. But "it happened" that Francis II died without issue and the link between France and Scotland was severed. . . .

'It is precisely when Britain is in danger from invasion, or her liberties are threatened, or her religion, and frequently all three are bound together — it is at the very time when ruin seems to the bravest heart most inevitable, that we see emerging certain factors entirely beyond the control of men that somehow avert the danger, and, more strangely still, contribute to a security and prosperity greater than that possessed before the crisis. The England after the Armada was immensely greater than the England of Elizabeth's accession. Great Britain after the

Napoleonic wars was incalculably more powerful than before them....

'Napoleon's hate was really concentrated against Britain. He leagued the whole of Europe against her. Twice he attempted invasion. For this he enlisted all his gigantic resources.... But it could not be. No mortal power could invade England....

'No national pride can blind the race to the fact that Waterloo was a fortunate "accident."' (It rained the night before and stalled Napoleon's artillery.)

In retrospect the author recalls the battle of Crecy, 'where a small and dwindling army on its backward march to the coast took its stand against the immeasurably superior numbers of the chivalry of France, and where the day was decided by an opportune storm of rain which so slackened the crossbows of the Genoese bowmen that they were unable to oppose their fire to that of the English archers, who had providentially protected their weapons.' (And more instances to the same effect.)

(About thirty years ago I became deeply interested in the great Russian Rezánov and wrote a novel about him as well as a biographical sketch for the Encyclopaedia Britannica. It was the intention of this remarkable and far-seeing man to present the whole Pacific Coast to Russia, by the peaceful method of sending out large numbers of Russian emigrants. The race is an extraordinarily fertile one, and no doubt would have multiplied so rapidly that they would have swarmed from the Columbia River to the frontier of Mexico before the small group of states on the eastern seaboard heard of the invasion; and the Pacific Coast would either be Russian today or the United States, at some later date, would have risked a war with Russia by sending an army to drive them out. Speculation is fruitless.

Everything seemed to favor Rezánov, who, in 1806, visited what is now San Francisco to obtain farinaceous foodstuffs for the scurvy-ridden colony at Alaska. It was a beneficent chance for his personal happiness that he really fell in love with the beautiful Concha Argüello, daughter of the most powerful man in Spanish California, but there is no doubt he would have wooed and won her in any case, for the friendship of those in possession, few in number as they were, was necessary to his great scheme.

And why was this great plan, with all signs so propitious, not carried out? This man of indomitable energy and iron will perished miserably of fever and hardships on his homeward journey through Siberia. The Spanish Californians were too feeble to make any resistance to the invading Americans later in the century. Certainly the Anglo-Saxon race, whether 'chosen' or not, has astonishing luck.)

Several chapters are devoted to the many afflictions visited upon England (as a matter of discipline, no doubt), such as successive ravages of the Plague, the War of the Roses and similar internal blights including the monarchical absolutism of Henry VIII and Bloody Mary; 'so foreign to the spirit of the race'; the struggles and triumphs of the Reformation; a frank admission of England's many mistakes, and of her unjust oppression of Ireland; her genius for colonization, which today leaves practically nothing for other nations to annex — and the author proceeds to sum up:

'A race filling the earth with a multitudinous people; dominating the seas; controlling the world's gates; unmolested in its possessions, as it was in its original home; its development directed and signalized by what is best explained as the especial favor — for some reason — of the Ruler of the Universe; its racial character marked by a love of freedom, a respect for law' (the author kindly omits all mention of the United States in this paragraph), 'a natural inclination to justice, truthfulness, and pity; a race that believes itself responsible for the world, and which has done much to alleviate suffering, to assist the helpless, and to spread the knowledge of the Gospel; yet marked by one blemish, one dissonant note' (presumably her treatment of Ireland) ' ... thus may we delineate the Anglo-Saxon race. The adventitious circumstances of power and dominion may be separated from the inherent characteristics, yet they are the result of those characteristics plus the mysterious good fortune which we have so frequently been forced to take into account, and therefore must be included in the portrait of the race. ...

'We are now face to face with a phenomenon of which we have ascertained the leading facts, and it is strange if our curiosity is not keenly aroused. How it originated is the first question that naturally occurs... and above all why should this race be signalized for such a preference?'...

2

'Had the race any previous experience in the dim forgotten past of a settled and civilized existence in which that well-known respect for law and constitutional authority was graven upon its yet plastic character, while by some happy chance it was trained in the exercise of an independence of self-expression which knew only the restraint of justice toward others?...

'We come to another fact that lies to our hand.... Just such a race, bearing exactly the characteristic marks that distinguish the Anglo-Saxon, was forecast and delineated ages ago; centuries before Caesar invaded Britain, a millennium before the Angles and Saxons and their kin settled in England.... The race thus predicted is to have a multitudinous posterity; it should spread over the earth; it should obtain all the strategic points of vantage against its enemies — picturesquely expressed in the language of that day as possessing "the gate of its enemies"; this multitudinous and dominating race was to have the aspect of "a nation and a community of nations," or, as it is again expressed, it was to be distinguished by being composed of two great branches, a great people on the one hand, and a company of nations on the other.... Again, this future race was to be established in a land where it would not be afflicted by the invasion of enemies, as it had repeatedly been afflicted in the earlier part of its history. This land ... is indicated as *a group of islands*, and again it is indicated as being in a direction northwest from the place where the predictions were uttered. Thus happily situated, the race, at first few in numbers, and very weak, was to renew its strength until it became the chief of the nations ... it should derive great wealth both from sea and land, it should inherit the empty spaces of the earth, it should cause deserts to become fertile and to "blossom like the rose." Finally this race was to have perpetual trouble, "thorns in the sides and pricks in the eyes" ... these thorns and pricks were to be members of an entirely different race which had been its enemy in the past.'

(Well, here we are!)

To quote is best. 'These predictions are made of Israel, *not of the Jews*. Let us clear the ground right here by pointing out the importance of this distinction. The Jews are the descendants of Judah, only *one* of the twelve tribes of Israel; consequently anything predicated of Israel, or the whole race, can no more be said to be predicated of the Jews than Yorkshire can be made to stand as an equivalent for all England. But more than this. Certain events occurred in the history of Israel which had the effect of separating Judah from the rest of Israel; obviously then many things may be true of Israel that do not apply to the Jews, just as, since the secession of the United

States, many things are true of the British Empire that are not true of the United States.'

After tracing the descent of the Saxons from the Sakai, who 'were Khumri, and the Khumri were the people known to us as the ten-tribed House of Israel,' the author, concluding a summary of certain other phases, remarks: 'Somehow, somewhere, the Anglo-Saxon race — or that race which we now call the Anglo-Saxon — was submitted to some plan of selection, some course of discipline, which has resulted in the characteristics now typical of the race, and, we repeat, typical of the race when it first comes into view.... Now, the world does possess the record of one race thus definitely selected and trained. That people are known as Israel and that record is to be found in the Bible.... We have seen that the predictions regarding Israel are one and all being fulfilled in the Anglo-Saxon race. We have seen that an historical connection has been traced by reputable scholars.' (The author has quoted Sharon Turner in his 'History of the Anglo-Saxons,' Rawlins's 'Heroditus,' and made certain allusions to Pliny.) 'If we can now find in the history of Israel a satisfactory reason and origin for those racial traits which are so amazingly persistent down the generations, we shall be forced by three-fold evidence to the conclusion that the Anglo-Saxon race and Israel are one....

'No fact is more awkward than that apparently there has been no fulfillment of the glowing promises recorded as being made to Israel by the Almighty. Apparently the race of Israel which starts out with such lofty claims, professing to be originated and developed under the fostering care of God Himself for some great purpose... this race has been dispersed and all but exterminated, it has become the subject of almost universal fear and aversion.... Apparently the only logical, the only reverent way out of the difficulty lies in believing that such great promises were not actually authentic, they were imagined by "the Jews" in their national pride and struggle for existence.

'But of course if the Anglo-Saxon race is really Israel, as it were risen from the dead, then we see the promises have been and are being fulfilled, and this objection with all its extensive implications collapses to the ground.... We propose therefore briefly to re-read the records, taking them literally and as they stand, to see whether they do not tell the whole story of a race originated and developed for a certain purpose. The whole story, the early part of it being written as history, the latter part as prophecy, necessarily because the records close ages before the second part was developed. *"This people have I formed for Myself; they shall show forth my praise."* Isaiah xliii, 21.

'Whatever may be our view of the Bible,' continues the author, 'whether we take the "modernist" or the "traditional" view, we must agree that as the arrangement stands, a remarkably orderly development of plot is represented which has a race for its hero.' After pointing out that the leading character when the story opens is Abram, the first arresting quotation is from Genesis xii, 1: 'Now the Lord God had said to Abram' (while he was still in Ur), '"Get thee out of thy country, and from thy kindred, and from thy father's house, unto a land that I will show thee; and I will make of thee a great nation." '

3

Ur of the Chaldees was a stronghold of idolatry. Abram was selected to establish the worship of the true God in another land 'before it becomes absolutely lost to men.'... 'There (in Canaan) under the especial care and tutelage of God a race should be developed that should become the guardians and eventually the distributors of the knowledge of the one true God. The story of Abraham may now be seen in its tremendously vital importance....'

It is not necessary to recount the vicissitudes by which Abram was tried and by no means found wanting, until he increased in wealth, 'in cattle, in silver, and in gold.' Also, his character develops into a striking family likeness to the highest type of British and Americans, a likeness stressed by the author later on.

But the time came when he reminded the Lord of His promise to make of him 'a great nation.' He and his wife Sarai are getting on, and no child has been born to them. The Almighty takes His time, but — 'when Abram was ninety years old and nine the Lord appeared to Abraham.... And God said to Abraham (whose name He had just changed): "As for Sarai thy wife thou shalt not call her name Sarai, but Sarah shall her name be. And I will bless her and give thee a son also of her; yea, I will bless her and she shall become a mother of nations; kings of people shall be of her." Then Abraham fell on his face and laughed and said in his heart, "Shall a child be born unto him that is an hundred years old? And shall Sarah, that is ninety years old, bear?" Genesis xvii, 15–17.'

Abraham's ribald humor refutes those interpreters of Holy Writ who contend that the Biblical computation of time differed from ours. Abraham was the father of English humor, which even Will Rogers pronounced deeper and more subtle than ours.

And probably no one has ever been more astonished than Abraham was when that promise was fulfilled and Sarah brought forth Isaac.

Saith the author: '*The great race that was to fill the earth was rooted in a miracle*, "so that there even sprang of one, and him as good as dead, so many as the stars of the sky in multitude, and as the sand which is by the seashore innumerable" is the inspired comment in Hebrews xi, 12.

'But while the miraculous race fitly begins its career in a miracle we may note with interest that precisely here occurs the condition that is apparently essential to the origination of a new race. Notwithstanding the belief in the potency of environment that existed a generation ago, modern science is more than doubtful whether any environmental conditions can produce essential variations in race; but should there arise a "mutation," or, as gardeners call it, a "sport," this by skillful care may be made the foundation of a distinct variety or breed. In the birth of Isaac, we suggest, just such a condition is found. But however that may be, what was more important, God was triumphantly revealed as the promise-fulfilling God. In the process, of course, Abraham had been proved. His faith and loving confidence in his Divine Helper had never really wavered, but in the main it was God who had been proved, not Abraham.'

Then came the supreme test of Abraham. God commanded him to take this worshipped child of his old age, as well as 'the one slender link upon which all the dreams of a great and wonderful posterity depend,' up to Mount Morah and lay him upon the altar of sacrifice. Abraham stood even this test, and at the last moment a ram was substituted and Isaac spared. 'Abraham has proved his right to become the "father of all them that believe."'... The sacrifice is the seed of the covenant.'

'And the Angel of the Lord called unto Abraham out of Heaven a second time and said, "By myself have I sworn, saith the Lord, for because thou hast done this thing, and hast not withheld thy son, thine only son; that in blessing I will bless thee, and in multiplying I will multiply thy seed as the stars of heaven, and as the sand which is upon the seashore; and thy seed shall possess the gate of his enemies; and in thy seed shall all nations of the earth be blessed because thou hast obeyed my voice."'

Referring to the earlier covenant, depicted in

Genesis xv: 'It is in direct answer to Abraham's inquiry: "Lord God, whereby shall I know that I shall inherit it?" . . . it has definite limitations, it is connected with the land in which the race is to be moulded and disciplined ere it can extend to the wider heritage destined for it. . . . But the covenant confirmed by the solemn oath of Jehovah is unlimited in scope, it is ratified in the clear light of day, and in the presence of a sacrifice that had taken Isaac's place upon the altar. . . . The first covenant indicates the first section of Israel's history, under the law; the second points to her history under grace when she arises as one from the dead and in gradual process of time inherits the spacious promises that the new covenant guarantees. . . .

'The world has seen only one race in which the principle, so general as to be received as a law of Nature — that prosperity inevitably tends to moral decline as surely as ripe fruit at once begins to decay — is suspended from action and its doom reversed. From the year 1800 the Anglo-Saxon race entered upon a heritage of unparalleled prosperity, yet never did material gain proceed more closely with spiritual aims. Missionary societies were formed, rulers acquired a new sense of responsibility to the weak, slaves were set free, prisoners relieved, evil social conditions were attacked by scores of leading men and women burning with indignation and pity' (and much more to the same effect).

Isaac had two sons. Esau was worthless and Jacob nothing to brag about until he repented of the sins of his youth and was rewarded by 'the Angel' with the name of Israel, Prince with God. In Jacob's son Joseph we have what might be called a reincarnation of Abraham, for his were all the virtues now peculiar to the Anglo-Saxon race (the best of them). 'As with Abraham, his character is strangely familiar, until we recognize that it is the very prototype of our racial heroes, our Alfred of England and Bruce of Scotland, our Hampdens, Cromwells, Washingtons, Lincolns, Lawrences, and Havelocks.... Joseph had realized all the ideal qualities at which the experiment aimed, a good and scientific reason for the preference given to his two sons sprung from so promising a stock... we cannot but recognize that the Anglo-Saxon race is distinguished by these very qualities to an exceptional degree which had their first inflorescence in Joseph.'

(More and more proofs, details and comparisons, which must be skipped.)

'The family has expanded into a race. No longer is it possible for so numerous a people to be guided by the simple rule imposed by the head of the tribe. As we know from familiar examples, heredity is only one factor in the art of breeding a distinctive race. Training or discipline is the other factor. It was perfectly possible that the family of Jacob might have been separated, as Ishmael and Esau had done, from the main stem. To prevent this, and also to receive the necessary discipline, the young race is led into Egyptian servitude.'

We skip the painful Egyptian experience.

'The next event to occur as soon as the nation had safely got beyond all danger from Egypt was the imposition of the Law. Law is the backbone — the bone structure — of any association of people for any purpose whatever. Consequently, as we might expect, the giving of the constitution was the first task of the leader Moses, or rather of the Divine Power of which Moses was the servant. Amid sounds and sights the most terrible and awe-inspiring, in order to imprint the solemnity of the occasion upon the careless minds of the people, there came first the majestic announcement of their Guide: "I am the Lord thy God which have brought thee out of the land of Egypt, out of the house of bondage." The people were then given those ten brief "words" that epitomize all the duty of man. These are followed by certain amplifications for the further regulation of social life. And, significantly, so far from beginning with the privileged classes, these laws open with regulations concerning the lowest class of all. Justice and humanity were thus in every sentence of the law instilled into the new race, contrary to the impression current today which has been formed by special instances of severity torn from their places and connection with an illogicality and disregard of historical perspective of which Bible history has been the peculiar victim. . . . We can only for the purposes of this inquiry select two principles that especially contributed to building up the sturdy independence of the individual, and that genius for self-government by which the nation of Israel became distinguished from its neighbors. The first

is expressed in the law of inheritance of the Land,'
Lev. xxv, 25–57.

(The idea apparently being that the land was the
common property of all men and if certain influential
men became great landowners, in due course the land
would be restored to the people. Witness the recent
breaking-up of great estates in England. The author
intimates that this condition is progressive.)

'The other factor in the development of Israel as a
free yet law-abiding race was the absence of a dominant central government and the committing of local
government to the people. Of the three functions of
government, the legislative, executive, and judicial,
the first at one stroke was virtually removed by the
Israelite constitution given at the creation of the
commonwealth. General principles were laid down
and so well illustrated by particular instances that it
was a body of law flexible enough to apply to all
future ages and developments. So comprehensive was
it that although monarchy was not introduced until
some centuries afterward, in the original constitution
the laws were already provided by which the king was
to be governed.... By the provision of an original
body of law an immense burden was removed from
the shoulders of the people. We may judge of this
by remembering the enormous amount of time that
is spent in self-governing countries upon law-making.
Were the necessity for this removed government would
be greatly simplified..... There remained the executive and judicial functions. Both were as broadly
distributed as possible; caring for the community

welfare, the adjustment of disputes, the administration of justice, even local defence, rested with the assembly of ''the Elders'' whose meeting place was the gate of the village or town. . . . A convincing illustration that demonstrates the operations of both these institutions — that of inheritance of the land and of local self-government — centuries after the nation had adopted monarchical government, is depicted in I Kings xxi.' (Here follows the story of Jezebel's attempt to convince her husband that the power of a king is absolute. — 'Dost thou now not govern the Kingdom of Israel?' — and was obliged to resort to bribery of the elders as she could not carry out her nefarious purpose by constitutional means.)

Contrast such a nation of free men with the surrounding nations. Everywhere but in Israel the system of government was an absolute monarchy, the monarch virtually possessing the lives and property of his subjects. . . . It is precisely this capacity for self-government which had been developed by *divinely* wise laws and centuries of exercise, that was the priceless heritage that Israel was able to hand down to its latest posterity. . . . *In Israel may be seen the one and only perfect state.*

4

But the Lord had created human nature, and doubtless for reasons of His own He permitted it to take its natural course. Theocracy degenerated into absolute monarchy, 'And the third king of the Davidic dynasty is scarcely enthroned before the nation divides itself into unequal parts... the Northern Kingdom, or Kingdom of Israel, is ruled by a succession of brief dynasties and its history is really the history of the struggle of Israel's God and the gods of the heathen for supremacy in the heart of Israel. Great prophets battle manfully for the God of Israel, the God who, they remind the people, brought them out of Egyptian slavery and made them a people and a nation....' .

Either to make them suffer for their sins or to test them further, Assyria, who was subjugating one nation after another, finally invaded Israel. 'Again and again the scourge of foreign enemies swept through the beloved land, the retreating tide bearing with it at different times the population of one district after another.... At length the end came. Samaria, the capital, after a desperate resistance, as may be judged by a siege three years long, was taken and the whole House of Israel was deported to other parts of the Assyrian dominion. This final catastrophe occurred in 721 B.C.... The southern kingdom, the kingdom of the House of Judah, held out longer, but in 585 B.C. fell to Nebuchadnezzar, King of Babylon, which had now risen upon the ruins of the Assyrian Empire, and all but the humblest of the land were deported to Babylon.'

The author exclaims: 'Yet we pause aghast. Is it possible — is it believable that we have been led all this way to arrive at such an end as this? The lines of the magnificent drama have been laid with supreme art, the opening scenes have been crammed with significance, promising to sweep on to a climax beyond the utmost dreams of human imagination — then the lines falter, become incoherent, and the drama is suddenly cut short, together with all the gorgeous promise that has so deeply thrilled the anticipation. Is it possible that this is the end? Or can we conceive it possible that the Omnipotent God should be frustrated in a design to which He had devoted His most watchful care? What then becomes of His covenanted promises?'

After disposing of the various interpretations of Biblical scholars who have sought to explain the seeming inconsistency or fickleness of the Almighty, and once more drawing a parallel between the Anglo-Saxon race and Israel at its best, we arrive by degrees at the author's own interpretation.

'But first let us reassert that Israel though exiled is not extirpated. The prophecy of Jeremiah is testimony to this. Jeremiah lived during the closing years of the Kingdom of Judah, witnessing its fall under Zedekiah the last king. This occurred one hundred and thirty-six years after the House of Israel had been deported, yet the prophecy of Jeremiah is full of references to this exiled House. Thus in chapter iii, 11, 12, he records: "The Lord said unto me 'The backsliding Israel hath justified itself more than treacherous Judah. Go and proclaim these words toward the North, and say Return thou backsliding Israel, saith the Lord.' "... And in Leviticus xxvi: "And yet for all that when they be in the land of their enemies I will not cast them away, neither will I abhor them, to destroy them utterly and to break my covenant with them; for I am the Lord their God. But I will for their sake remember the *covenant of their ancestors*.''

Then Israel is specifically told, adds the author: 'Thou art my battle-axe and weapons of war; for with thee will I break in pieces the nations, and with thee will I destroy kingdoms.'

Saith the author: 'Now, since we know that the Judah section did not become a battle-axe and destroy kingdoms, it is evidently the ten-tribed House of Israel that avenged upon Babylon the sorrows of Jerusalem. Babylon fell in 538 B.C. What happened in that period of one hundred and eighty-three years that enabled a nation of captives to renew their strength and take part against Babylon in company with the Medes and the Persians? That Israel was a remarkably vigorous race we know, and it is evident that they multiplied with at least as great rapidity as during their former captivity in Egypt. If this was so the few hundred thousands that had settled in their place of exile had increased to millions. Then, very soon after their deportation the Assyrian Empire began to decline. The Assyrians found, as all nations warring against Israel have found — as Spain, France, Holland, and Germany have found in the days of Israel's renascence — that there is something fatal in so doing. And Israel with its strong instinct for freedom would not be slow in throwing off the bonds. So the second book of Esdras records that some of the people of Israel, crossing the upper reaches of the Euphrates, left the sphere of the Assyrian Empire and travelled for a year and a half to Ar-sareth, which has abundantly been identified as being the district situated between the Danube and the Dneister, where many Hebrew relics and inscriptions have been found. But while a section of the Israelites thus departed, there is evidence that a great number remained in the vicinity of Assyria and became celebrated under the title of Sakai.'

Much history must be skipped here, including the crushing defeats inflicted by the Sakai upon powerful tribes, as we are interested only in the identification of Israel with the Anglo-Saxon race.

Speaking of the lost tribes of Israel, bobbing up here and there under a new name: 'The physical vigour of the people, their impatience of any restraint save that imposed by their own will, yet their ability for acting together, a certain mercifulness of the free-hearted and unfearing — modified sometimes by a stern ruthlessness where injustice has been suffered — by such characteristics we would expect to identify them as we catch glimpses of them through the meagre records of that period. "For lo, I will command and I will sift [cause to move to and fro] the House of Israel among all the nations, like as corn is sifted in a sieve, yet shall not the least grain fall to the ground." Amos ix, 9, R.V.'

In Chapter IX, entitled 'The Fortunate Isles,' the author of 'The Wonder Race' clinches her argument with further quotations from the Bible. To begin with: 'The promise made by the Almighty to David in II Samuel vii, 10–11: "Moreover I will appoint a place for my people Israel, and will plant them, that they may dwell in a place of their own, and move no more." ... Two things are evident in this promise, first that the place must be far from the then sphere of the ambitions of great empires, secondly that it must have some great natural barrier.... This puts out of court the interpretation of some commentators that the "Isles" were coastlands. Palestine was a coastland and was doubly exposed to trouble on that very account. From Isaiah it is evident that the place where Israel would be "planted," where they would be no more afflicted by incursions of enemies, to repel which the judges were raised up in Israel, was to be in the "isles." Indeed where could such a place be if not in an island or islands?'

References to the isles and islands are quoted liberally from Isaiah. 'The forty-first chapter opens with "Keep silence (or keep concealed) before me, O islands; and let the people renew their strength." How the people of the British Isles, few in number at first, have renewed their strength all the world knows. The forty-second chapter, after referring to that Servant who should fulfill all the will of God, says: "He shall not fail nor be discouraged, till he have set judgment on the earth: *and the isles shall wait for his law*." And in the tenth verse, "Sing unto the Lord a new song, and His praise from the end of the earth, ye that go down to the sea and all that is therein, *the isles and the inhabitants thereof*.... Let them give glory unto the Lord and *declare his praise in the islands*."

In the forty-ninth chapter the isles are informed of the coming of the Servant who represents Israel, who is to restore the preserved of Israel. . . . Once more, in Isaiah li, 5, the Prophet, specifically addressing Israel, says: "My righteousness is near; my salvation is gone forth, and mine arms shall judge the people; *the isles shall wait upon me* and on mine arm shall they trust." A mass of evidence like this is overwhelmingly conclusive that in some way some islands were to be closely associated with Israel in her redeemed and restored state. That these islands were identical with the place of rest promised to David is certain.'

The many physical advantages over any other islands of what are now known as the British Isles, to say nothing of the position indicated, are dwelt upon, and the author proceeds to demolish the claim of the Phoenicians to be the very first to discover England, although the Phoenicians made many excursions in company with the Israelites, and quotes Hannay's 'Eur. and O. R. Origins' as evidence that a school of thought is 'growing up' which sees it was Israel and not Phoenicia that was the first in those explorations now associated with the Phoenician name, and it was only after the downfall of Israel that Phoenicia was able to appropriate the glory and credit of the enterprise. Also, many quotations from Judges, Chronicles, Psalms, to bear this out. (It may as well be said here that the Irish, being largely descended from Phoenician colonists, are supposed for that reason to be the hereditary enemies of the English race. Hardly of the Anglo-Saxon race in general, for they certainly get along well with Americans, and the older immigrants are now part of the American pattern.)

But let the author continue. 'Thenceforward toward this new land of promise the race slowly gathered. When David's line was cut off at the fall of Jerusalem and the sons of Zedekiah were slain before his eyes, the King's daughters were assigned to the care of the Prophet Jeremiah, who, it will be remembered, was commissioned to root out and pull down, *to build up and plant*. For thirty-nine sorrowful years the Prophet had uttered the message of doom, now he was to enter upon his joyous task to build and to plant. He was accompanied by Baruch the scribe. Knowing now the commercial enterprise of that day, knowing that Nebuchadnezzar had sent colonies of Jews to Spain, it is not difficult to see that Jeremiah and his companions also went to the west. The story is taken up in Ireland, where it is known that a great Prophet with a scribe named "Brug" and a king's daughter arrived there. This princess married the over-King of Ireland. She is evidently the "tender twig" taken from the topmost branch, i.e., the last King of Judah, and "planted in the mountain of the height of Israel," or in the place where Israel would become great — for mountains stand for national power in prophetic symbology — as prophesied in Ezekiel xvii. Absolutely nothing is more certain than that the line of David continued unbroken, for David's throne was to endure for ever, though if the heirs of that throne sinned they would be punished and another of the royal line would take the throne. This is illustrated again and again in the royal House of Britain. There have been succeeding dynasties but they have all been connected by blood, and these connecting links have been *women*, daughters of the reigning House that, like Zedekiah's daughter, preserved the continuity and provided the heir when he was required. Thus the sister of Edgar Atheling married Malcolm of Scotland, in whose veins flowed the blood of the Irish kings descended from the daughter of Zedekiah and the Heremon or King of Ireland.' (More and more instances, quoted in part from Milner's 'Royal House of Britain,' which need not be given here.)

'In other countries dynasty has succeeded dynasty with *no blood connection;* in Britain there has been one enduring line since the beginning of history. The rational explanation is that Israel, restored to a new life in the Isles, has its throne of David to reign over it, as Jeremiah (xxxiii, 17) assures us: "For thus saith the Lord, David shall never want a man to sit upon the throne of Israel." This is highly significant. It is the House of Israel, not the House of Judah, over which David's descendants from Rehoboam to Zedekiah reigned. *"Where the House of Israel is there must be David's throne."* ... It is still an earthly throne and still occupied by a son of David.' (References to II Samuel, Psalm xxxiv, Jeremiah xxxiii.)

(Query: Is David watching over a certain namesake of his?)

5

It may be as well to interpolate here that in the Encyclopaedia Britannica there is a brief paragraph about a man named Brothers (1757–1824) who advanced much the same theory (although it is doubtful if he distinguished the House of Israel from the House of Judah), and even wanted to lead the Anglo-Saxon race back to Canaan, but as the man was a lunatic one wonders why he is thought worthy of being immortalized in the Britannica. Possibly because he obtained two million enthusiastic followers among the Jews, who had obtained their first real foothold in Britain in the seventeenth century. The Pundit who writes the paragraph dismisses the 'Anglo-Israelite theory' as historically and etymologically unsound. As to the last, he forgets that while the small remnant of Jews returned to Palestine after seventy years of exile and remained there, the Israelites were scattered over Europe, and, it is more than likely, abandoned for convenience' sake their original language. Certainly their descendants would know little or nothing of it. As to the history of both races, it was left to a more careful student of the Bible to make the modern theory plausible.

So, let us keep to our muttons.

The author continues. 'We have seen how Israel became dispersed through all countries, at times waxing great, and wielding the sword of Jehovah's judgments against guilty nations, and again diminished and brought low. For the punishment foretold by

Moses must extend over a weary period of years, yet characterized by an ebb and flow, a rise and fall in intensity.'

It is the author's theory that they finally concentrated in Normandy, Anglia, Saxonia, Jutland, and Denmark, or had settled among previous inhabitants and absorbed them, 'breeding out' the original stock. The same may be said of the 'ancient Britons.'

We must turn back the pages of history for a moment.

Christ had come and His religion was battling with the deeply rooted paganism of Europe. 'The consensus of opinion in the Church of Rome is that in Britain was established the first national Church. Early Christian fathers agree that the light of the Gospel had spread to Britain *far beyond those districts penetrated by the Roman arms*, and in A.D. 314 three British bishops were present at the Council of Arles. British bishops were also present at the great Council of Nicea in 325.'

Now, as the Angli invasion of Britain was in the fifth century A.D., the Saxon in the fourth, that of the Danes and Jutes in the fifth, and the Normans in the eleventh, and as King Caractacus of Britain in the first century was taken to Rome with his family and held Christian services in his house, it stands to reason that if the 'Ancient Britons' sent bishops to Arles in the early years of the fourth century they could hardly have been savages, but intelligent and educated Israelites who opened their minds to the new religion, their inherited traditions and instincts making them naturally among the first converts.

Or to quote the author: 'For in it lies the incontro-
vertible proof that our ancestors for themselves and
their descendants received the redemption long before
promised through Christ and immediately gave proof
of not only the vigour of their faith, but the fact of
their being really Israel by at once beginning to be
witnesses for God. We quote again from the learned
Bishop Stubbs:

'"Europe was still for the most part unconverted;
in France bishops and clergy were ambitious, venal,
and immoral; the state of Italy was little better; that
of Spain was still worse with its Arian heresy. In
Germany heathenism practically prevailed almost
everywhere, the whole of the north and centre was as
heathen as it had been in the time of Caesar." (Heil
Hitler!) "During this age the Church of England was
the light of the western world.... Thus the whole of
the northwest and centre of Europe owes its Christianity to English missions."'

Of course the point we are to get is this: The religion
of Christ is a religion of peace on earth and good-will
to men. The Israelites, converging by degrees into
the islands until finally they formed a homogeneous
race, later to be known as the Anglo-Saxon, were to
be a world power whose watchword would be peace,
not war; which should, in fact, reverse all the received
ideas attaching to world-empire, regarding dominions
as responsibilities, not privileges, and leadership as
the opportunity for service.

Well, England has had a few wars on her own, but
it must be admitted that for many years now she has

done her best to act as peacemaker and avert war, and she certainly exercises no tyranny over her dominions. The secession of the United States taught her a lesson, and, it must be remembered, it was her misfortune at that time to be ruled by a stupid German king with a yen to restore monarchical despotism. Many of the most eminent in Great Britain openly avowed their sympathy with the rebellious colonies.

The author has her own explanation. 'The separation of the United States was as inevitable as all the decrees of the Almighty must be, and such a separation had been decreed since the day when the patriarchal Jacob told Joseph that one of his sons would be a "great people" while the other would be a "multitude of nations." '

That England's sense of justice is the most highly developed in the world today no one will honestly deny; that is to say, no one who is a dispassionate student of history past and current. Her great fault is that she sometimes hesitates too long. If the British Lion had emitted a mighty roar a little earlier in 1914 the Germanic knee might have wobbled and the World War been averted.

The author makes another interesting point. 'Sir Lawrence Gomme shows in his "Governance of London" that the Roman occupation was limited to the Roman cities in Britain, the Britons remaining unassimilated. When the foreign influence was gone nothing remained of its institutions. Instead it is evident from the ancient British laws and customs that it is to them we owe many of the elements of our common law. The English inherited *nothing* from the Roman occupation either in law, language, or custom. This is in marked contrast to the continent. . . . The famous Roman Law is the law of the continent of Europe to this day. The English, rich in their own "common law," inherited no part of the Roman Law from its first settlement, and only accepted a few scientific and professional axioms at a later period.'

The author cherishes no delusion as to the Anglo-Saxon race having reached a state of perfection. She laments its alcoholic tendencies. ('The drink bill in the United Kingdom in 1922 was 354,131,000 pounds, and the total consumption approximately 53,500,000 gallons.') And that the United States, while making alcoholic liquor illegal, was becoming enslaved to narcotic drugs. She lashes Great Britain for her many other delinquencies, including her decline in Faith. 'We know how far we are from the dreams of Utopia.' Being intensely religious her only hope lies in a universal return to the Fold, of submission to the God of Israel, and universal good behavior. Ah, Utopia!

Well, there it is, this curious and interesting theory of the Wonder Race. Take it or leave it.

THE END